Political Ethics

*AN APPLICATION OF ETHICAL PRIN-
CIPLES TO POLITICAL RELATIONS*

BY

DANIEL SOMMER ROBINSON

PROFESSOR OF PHILOSOPHY
INDIANA UNIVERSITY

THOMAS Y. CROWELL COMPANY
PUBLISHERS · NEW YORK

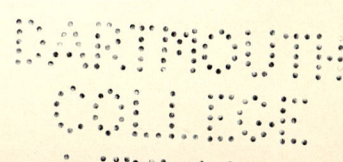

To my own and all other students who are privileged to possess, to conserve, and to enhance the cultural values transmitted to them by the higher educational institutions of a free people

COPYRIGHT, 1935
BY THOMAS Y. CROWELL COMPANY

All rights reserved. No part of this book may be reproduced in any form except by a reviewer who may quote brief passages in a review to be printed in a magazine or newspaper.

PRINTED IN THE UNITED STATES OF AMERICA BY
J. J. LITTLE AND IVES COMPANY, NEW YORK

PREFACE

The purpose of this book is explained in the brief introduction. Here I need only add that I hope that my discussions may prove stimulating to the general reader, and useful to teachers of political and elementary ethics, government and social civics courses, and to leaders of discussion groups conducted under the auspices of such organizations as the International Relations Club, the Y. M. C. A., Public Forums, Churches, and Extension and Evening Schools.

This is a pioneer textbook that has been made possible by a number of pioneer treatises and essays on political relations since the World War. Inasmuch as most of these writings are listed in the reading lists at the end of each chapter, it is not necessary to name any of them here. Readers who wish to delve more deeply into the problems discussed herein are advised to make use of these carefully selected references. Teachers should assign one or more special topics to each student for oral or written reports, based upon a careful study of certain of these and other original sources.

The only hope that a moral world order may ultimately replace the dog eat dog policy, which today dominates so many of the men of action who are responsible for administering the affairs of nations, lies in the creation of a body of world opinion well enough organized to exert a strong influence on the statesmen of all nations. The author trusts that many of the younger generation of citizens of the United States may find that the discussions in this book are genuinely informative, that they help to clarify the deep issues involved in the relation of each youth to his own state, and that they aid in answering some of the perplexing questions arising from the relations of the various peoples of the earth to each other, in this age when world politics are so enormously complicated and so overwhelmingly important. For even a partial attainment of these ends would be a slight contribution to the formation and crystallization of that kind of world opinion which is the indispensable condition of the making of a more ethical world order.

I am indebted to my students, especially Mr. Paul Leon Butze, Mr. J. Morton-Finney and Mrs. Miriam Yellen, to my colleagues, Professors Velorus Martz, Stephen S. Visher and Hugh E. Willis, and to my wife for helpful suggestions. My typist, Miss Mae Fishback, has assisted me in many ways. It will be obvious to the reader that I owe much to the instruction and writings of my esteemed teacher and friend, Professor William Ernest Hocking, whose numerous contributions to social and political philosophy I believe to be of epoch making significance.

TABLE OF CONTENTS

PREFACE   vii

INTRODUCTION   xiii

I. A DEFINITION OF POLITICAL ETHICS   1
1. Applied Ethics Differentiated from Theoretical Ethics
2. A Traditional Classification of the Problems of Applied Ethics
3. Critical Examination of the Traditional Classification
4. A Reconstruction of the Traditional Classification to Correct These Defects
5. A Definition of Political Ethics. Delimitation of its Subject Matter

II. WHY THERE ARE STATES   22
1. The Child's Conception of the State
2. Stages in the Development of Social Consciousness
3. Hobbes and Rousseau Contrasted
4. Three Kinds of Evils Against Which Man Contends
   (1) The Clash of Ideals
   (2) The Competitive Nature of Economic Value
   (3) The Fixity of Institutions
5. How to Deal With These Evils

III. THE POSTULATES OF AN IDEAL STATE   44
1. Explanation of Terminology
2. The Postulate of Identical Ideals

3. The Postulate of the Transformation of Competitive into Non-Competitive Interests
4. The Postulate of Constructive Criticism
5. The Postulate of Conserving Force
6. Five Jural Postulates

IV. THE THREE ORDERS OF AN IDEAL STATE   64

1. The Private Order
2. The Public Order
3. Relations of the Public and Private Orders to Each Other
4. The Cultural Order
5. Relation of the Cultural to the Other Two Orders

V. CONFORMITY OF ACTUAL STATES TO THE IDEAL: THE SOVIET STATE   81

1. The Problem Stated
2. Difficulty of Judging the Soviet State
3. Opposing Interpretations of the Importance of the Soviet State
4. Application of the Four Postulates to the Soviet State
5. Application of the Three Orders to the Soviet State

VI. CONFORMITY OF ACTUAL STATES TO THE IDEAL: DICTATORSHIPS   105

1. Extent and Uniqueness of Contemporary Dictatorships
2. Difficulty of Applying the Postulates and Three Orders to Dictatorships
3. Application of the Four Postulates to Dictatorships
4. Application of the Three Orders to Dictatorships
5. General Conclusions

VII. CONFORMITY OF ACTUAL STATES TO THE IDEAL: REPRESENTATIVE DEMOCRACIES   129

1. The Extent and Importance of Representative Democracies

TABLE OF CONTENTS

2. Application of the Four Postulates to Representative Democracies
3. Application of the Three Orders to Representative Democracies
4. An Examination of Two Criticisms of Representative Democracies
5. General Conclusion

VIII. THE APPLICATION OF ETHICAL PRINCIPLES TO INTERNATIONAL RELATIONS — 155

1. Extent to Which Ethical Principles are Applicable to International Relations
2. The Ethical Queerness of States
   (1) Uniqueness of each state
   (2) The puzzles of identity
   (3) Property
   (4) Existence
   (5) Vital Interests
3. The First Approach to the Application of Ethical Principles to International Relations
4. The Second Approach to the Application of Ethical Principles to International Relations
5. The Gradual Actualization of the Idea of the Unity of Mankind

IX. CULTURAL MONISM VERSUS CULTURAL PLURALISM — 182

1. Explanation of Terminology
2. Cultural Monism
3. Cultural Pluralism
4. Applications of Cultural Monism and Pluralism to Current International Relations

X. THE MEASURES OF BACKWARDNESS — 203

1. Three Primary Measures of Backwardness
   (1) The Mastery of Nature
   (2) The General Level of Public Morality
   (3) The Condition of the Masses

TABLE OF CONTENTS

   2. Cultural Latency
   3. Other Measures of Backwardness
   4. A Provisional Classification of Peoples

XI. THE RIGHTS OF BACKWARD PEOPLE 224

   1. The Right of Conquest
   2. Economic Imperialism
   3. Cultural Values the Basis of Right
   4. How the Right to Self-Government is to be Determined

XII. THE NEW LEAGUE OF NATIONS 246

   1. Some Inherent Weaknesses in the League of Nations
   2. The Present Status of the League
   3. Mr. Baker's Solution of the Present Problem
   4. The Reconstruction of the League of Nations

CASES FOR DISCUSSION 266

INDEX 279

INTRODUCTION

Geologists tell us that there have occurred from time to time in the ages of earth's history gigantic and catastrophic cataclysms in which whole continents have been submerged beneath the waters of the trackless ocean. In the sphere of human events the World War is in many respects analogous to such cataclysms. It destroyed billions of dollars worth of property, including many priceless art treasures; slaughtered millions of youths before they had even entered the prime of life; maimed and shell-shocked other millions; left numberless children orphaned and countless young women either widowed or without hope of marriage; and brought as its aftermath the Russian, Italian, German and other minor revolutions and the economic depression, to say nothing of the burden of hatred and ill-will that will be extremely difficult to liquidate without more carnage. In short it completely upset the social, political, and economic equilibrium of all of the peoples of the earth.

Today in every land thinking people are deeply perturbed over what the future may have in store, not only for individual men and women and boys and girls, but for civilization and culture as a whole. They are asking whether any government can long endure, whether civilization itself may not now be disintegrating under the strain of post-war conditions, whether mankind may not have to face in the near future another world conflagration which will actually put an end to all ordered society and throw humanity back into a permanent condition of barbarism. Never before in human history have political relations been so overwhelmingly important for the welfare of all mankind as they are today. Never has it been so essential to determine from an ethical point of view what is the best form of government.

It is certainly an unfortunate, and it may be an ominous and portentous fact that the excessive departmentalizing of knowledge in higher institutions of learning should have led to a sharp separation of philosophy and politics just at this period when political relations are so stupendously significant. Politics have been assigned to the Department of Government, where the effort is frequently made to ban all political philosophizing in the interest of the ideal of making this branch of human knowledge strictly scientific. As a result too many courses in government slur over the basal issues of political philosophy, and emphasize excessively the minutiae of political organizations and their functioning. The primary aim of the Department of Government has come more and more to be the training of experts capable of performing efficiently the various functions of government. And this has been accompanied by a gradual subordination of the great problems of political philosophy to this purely utilitarian aim.

Contemporaneous with this trend in the study of politics has been the trend in the Department of Philosophy towards the divorce of ethics from politics. It is true that all of the great classical philosophers included political relations in the subject-matter of ethics. Thus Plato's *Republic* deals with both moral and political philosophy in our sense of the word; Aristotle's *Ethics* was written as an introduction to his *Politics;* in modern philosophy both Spinoza and Hobbes treated ethics and politics as inseparable, while Hegel, the most encyclopaedic of philosophers, gives no attention to ethics apart from his analysis of society found in the *Philosophy of Right.* Disregarding this fact, too many ethics textbooks of the recent past have been chiefly concerned with the great problems of ethical theory. Many pages are devoted to the history of morals and of ethics, and to the discussion of the nature and criteria of value and of duty, and of such ultimate issues as God, freedom, conscience, and immortality, and comparatively little space is left for a consideration of the vital questions of Applied Ethics.

In fact this division of ethics has not even been clearly defined. Certainly its wide scope has never been fully appreciated by authors of elementary ethics textbooks. For such space as they have seen fit to give to Applied Ethics has unusually been restricted to a discussion of casuistical disputes in the fields of Personal and Professional Ethics. Political relations have been almost completely ignored.

In his excellent *Elements of Ethics,* which was written some years before the World War, Professor J. H. Muirhead laments the fact that most recent writers in the field of ethics have so completely ignored political relations. In a note appended to his chapter entitled *The Scope of the Science of Ethics* he points out that the fashion of treating the problems of ethics and of politics apart from one another is "the result of temporary circumstances, and may be very misleading." Continuing, he wisely remarks: "The truth seems to be, that modern intuitionalism and modern hedonism (both, it is to be observed, forms of individualism and of English growth) are responsible for the present fashion of treating ethical questions in abstraction from their political correlatives. Finding as they do the principle of moral obligation in the individual mind, whether as the seat of "innate ideas" or the percipient of pain and pleasure, they have assigned to ethics, as its chief subject, the discussion of such questions as the nature of conscience and the freedom of the will. But it is every day becoming clearer that it is a mistake to look to what is purely individual in man as the ground of his moral judgments or the source of his prevailing motives, or even to conceive of the individual in any way as arbitrarily selecting the principles which are to guide his conduct. The motives under the influence of which each of us habitually lives are much more accurately represented by that mysterious confluence of impulses which we call the spirit of the age, and which, as consisting of elements borrowed from the present constitution of society, current ideas upon rights of person and property, and the prevailing conceptions of the end or purpose of social effort, it is the duty of social or political philosophy to analyze. When this is more generally acknowledged, it may be anticipated that the distinction in the text will again pass into the background, psychological questions will occupy a smaller, sociological and political a larger and more central place in ethical discussion." [1]

Surely this is a truly prophetic utterance. The time has undoubtedly already come when students of ethics should be taught to discuss intelligently the application of ethical principles to political relations. And more and more this is coming to be recognized by teachers of ethics. The fundamental purpose of this book is to provide suitable and sufficient material which can be used as a basis for such discussion. It will be necessary to begin by distinguishing briefly but carefully between morals and ethics and between Theoretical and Applied Ethics. This will enable us to place Political Ethics within the larger field of Applied Ethics and to indicate its wide scope. This is the task of the first chapter, which is intended to help pave the way for a consideration of the basic ethical principles of an ideal state which can be

[1] J. H. Muirhead *The Elements of Ethics*, 3rd. ed. 1910. (John Murray, Publisher.)

actualized, and for the evaluating of some leading actual states by using these principles as criteria or standards of measurement. But before attempting to set up such an ideal state it is also necessary to explain what the state is and why men need it in opposing the evils of life, and that is the purpose of the second chapter.

Chapters VIII-XI deal with the complicated problems involved in the relations between peoples and cultures. Obviously volumes have been and will be written on these problems. These chapters are preliminary and introductory. They merely aim to open up this important field for discussion. Some of the ideas in these chapters are original, but most of them are borrowed. From a philosophical point of view chapters VIII and IX are probably the most important in the book. Chapter VIII summarizes and applies Dr. A. N. Whitehead's recent ethical interpretation of West European history, an interpretation which richly deserves to become widely known. Chapter IX deals with opposed theories of culture and philosophies of history, including the theory of Oswald Spengler. Chapter XII contains an exposition of the League of Nations with which most educated American citizens will no doubt agree, at least, in general.

Thirty carefully selected Cases for Discussion are appended in the hope that they may prove suggestive to teachers and useful for classroom discussions.

CHAPTER I

A DEFINITION OF POLITICAL ETHICS

1. Applied Ethics Differentiated from Theoretical Ethics

There is an important distinction between morals and ethics which is frequently overlooked. This is partly because the distinction is difficult in itself and partly because making it involves taking a stand on the vexed problem of the nature of ethics. The word morals comes from the Latin word *mores,* which means customs and is sometimes used in English in its Latin form. Some customs are positive, that is to say, acts that the individual is permitted to do, and some are negative, acts forbidden. Tabus constitute the negative customs of savages, and they play an important rôle in regulating tribal behavior.

Now there is a type of ethics which is based upon the fundamental principle: "The mores make anything right." In other words, every custom that is actually practiced by a people is right for that people at the time that they observe it. On this view ethics is a purely descriptive science. Its function is to observe and describe the actual customs of human beings, and to trace their evolution from savage to civilized people. On this interpretation ethics is a positive natural science, just like biology. It uses the genetic method, that is to say, it traces customs to their genesis out of some environmental situation, and describes them in detail.

Such a conception of ethics is more inadequate than it is entirely fallacious. Great anthropologists and sociologists, such as Edward Westermarck and L. T. Hobhouse,[1] have made a permanent contribution to social science by systematic research into the tribal customs of various savages and lower races, by tracing the evolution of such customs, and by noting the way in which clan and tribal types of social organization are displaced by wider and wider groups and associations, and how customs are thereby changed. More popular writers have utilized this material effectively in telling the fascinating story of human morals or mores. Nevertheless there is a basic difference between ethics viewed as the description of customs and ethics viewed as the study and investigation of norms or principles of evaluating human conduct. What is that difference?

Suppose a thinker happens to raise the important question of why a particular custom is approved by his own group? Suppose he asks what such a custom means, what value it has, and whether some other practice might not conceivably be better? To put it quite generally, suppose he demands *reasons* for customs, reasons good enough to satisfy an intelli-

[1] See Edward Westermarck: *Origin and Development of Moral Ideas*, 2 vols., and L. T. Hobhouse: *Morals in Evolution*, 2 vols.

gent and reflective person? Such a demand, when carried through, will culminate in the adoption of some one principle, or some set of ideal standards, which can be used in evaluating customs. Such principles or standards are called *norms*. Note that a norm in ethics is a standard of value and not an average. There is no connection between the use of the word norm in statistics, where it means an average, and its use in ethics, where it means an ideal standard or principle which is used to evaluate human behavior.

When human beings reach the stage in cultural evolution where they can evaluate their own customs by applying norms or standards to them they are said to be in the stage of reflective morality. That is to say, their morality is based upon reflection as to the end or purpose of their actions, instead of being a mere blind adherence to custom. In spite of the fact that custom plays a large rôle in the lives of the highly civilized peoples, generally speaking their morality is reflective.

Consequently, by far the majority of writers on theoretical ethics hold that the subject is primarily a study of norms or principles of value, and is only secondarily concerned with a description of actual customs. Such thinkers reject the view that the main business of ethics is to trace the genesis and development of the mores. They hold that customs without norms are ethically meaningless, and they reject the basic norm of the sociological school that the mores make anything right. Customs do not give norms. Reflection is essential to their discovery. Ethics is restricted to the stage of reflective morality. Only in the most rudimentary sense can savages and the lower races of men be said to be ethical. Systematic ethical reflection is entirely absent among such peoples. It is found only among highly civilized modern peoples, and among such ancient peoples as the Chinese, Hindus, Hebrews, Persians, Greeks, and Romans. Consequently, an investigation of the ethical systems and ideas produced by the great sages of these cultures is of far greater importance to the study of ethics than is the study of the ways of savages, regardless of how interesting and valuable the latter may be.

This suggests the essential meaning, and the basic problems of *Theoretical Ethics*. This branch of human knowledge is constituted by a well knit set of norms or standards for evaluating human conduct and human customs. It seeks to determine the actual essence of value and of obligation and to express this essence in basic ethical laws or principles. Naturally ethical theorizers will reach different conceptions of what value and duty are. Consequently, there cannot be said to be just one system of theoretical ethics. Every philosopher knows that there are a number of different ethical systems, and every honest philosopher will admit that some of these systems are entirely consistent internally, and that they can be attacked only from the standpoint of some other system. Yet he must also admit that

DEFINITION OF POLITICAL ETHICS

theoretical ethics is constituted by a set of norms or standards.

Applied Ethics is the application of the principles or norms of theoretical ethics to concrete cases. These cases are the actual behavior, incipient or overt, of real moral agents. But what is a moral agent? As we shall see presently, the way in which this question is answered seriously affects the application of ethical principles. And the question is not easily answered. Moreover, in answering it one must resort to ethical theorizing. Thus we are in a dilemma. The extent to which ethical theory can be applied is largely determined by one's theory of the agent, so that when we begin to apply ethical theories we must resort to more theorizing. There is no escaping this dilemma, except by arbitrarily laying down one's own conception of what the field of applied ethics is. But before doing this it will be fairer and clearer to give the usual traditional classification of the problems of applied ethics.

2. A Traditional Classification of the Problems of Applied Ethics

Immanuel Kant classified the problems of philosophy under four major questions:

1. "Was kann ich wissen?"   What can I know?
2. "Was soll ich thun?"   What ought I to do?
3. "Was darf ich hoffen?"   What may I hope?
4. "Was ist der Mensch?"   What is man?

And he comments that the answer to the first question constitutes *Metaphysics*, that to the second

Ethics, that to the third *Religion,* and that to the fourth *Anthropology*.[2] This division of the problems of philosophy has been very influential, indeed it is generally regarded as one of the classic divisions.

We are here concerned with Kant's second question, which he took to be the central question of ethical theory. His own ethics is centered around that moral law which determines every man's obligations, and which he says is dictated to each individual by his own rational good will. To emphasize its binding character he called it the categorical imperative, and he stated it in three different ways: (1) "Act only on that maxim whereby thou canst at the same time will that it should become a universal law." (2) "So act as to treat humanity, whether in thine own person or in that of any other, in every case as an end withal, never as means only." (3) Consider "the will of every rational being as a universally legislative will."[3] In spite of its tendency towards a purely formalistic theory of ethics, Kant's categorical imperative is still recognized as one of the basic norms of ethics, and in the form of the principle that personality should be put above property it is also a recognized

[2] See Immanuel Kant: *Logik: Ein Handbuch zu Vorlesungen* (Königsberg, 1800), p. 25.

[3] Immanuel Kant: *Metaphysic of Morals,* Section II. Kant contrasted the categorical imperative with hypothetical or conditional imperatives, which he called "maxims of prudence," such as: "If one wants durable satisfaction, then he must abstain from excesses." Hypothetical imperatives are dictated by desires and inclinations, whereas the categorical imperative is dictated by one's moral good will, which Kant called the practical reason.

DEFINITION OF POLITICAL ETHICS

principle of law. We shall have occasion to refer to it again.

Other writers have added two more questions to the one question of Kant. These questions are: *What ought I to have?* and *What ought I to be?* These two questions are put with the one asked by Kant, and the three are called the basic questions of Practical Philosophy.[4] This gives three divisions of Applied Ethics: I. *The Doctrine of Human Rights*, in which the answer to the question *What ought I to have?* is given; II. *The Doctrine of Duties*, which answers Kant's question, and III. *The Doctrine of Virtues*, which answers the third question.

This traditional classification of the problems of applied ethics rests upon the basic assumption that *individual human beings are the only direct moral agents*. Groups are excluded from the class of direct moral agents by this assumption. Although it is admitted that groups initiate and carry out policies and are treated in municipal law[5] as "legal persons," nevertheless the individuals in the groups are the source of whatever morality there is in these actions and policies. A legal person is a fictitious being useful for the purposes of corporation and other forms of law, enabling individuals to escape responsibility for its actions, and yet incapable of acting save as its robotic arms are manipulated by the various real persons who created it and who

[4] See W. M. Urban: *Fundamentals of Ethics*, Chapter IX.
[5] The term *municipal law* as here used means all official formal regulations within a country, such as legislative statutes, executive orders, rescripts, ukases, and stands in contrast to *international law*.

maintain the steady tenor of its way. Individual human beings, and not groups, associations, and communities formed out of such real persons, are ultimately the only direct moral agents.

Now this assumption, upon which the traditional classification is based, carries with it an important and seemingly valid logical implication to the effect that ethical principles are applicable only to persons. This seems to follow directly from the assertion that individuals are the only direct moral agents. Thus the three problems of applied ethics are so formulated as to carry this implication in the very form in which they are stated. In practice, to be sure, writers who use the traditional classification refer to the rights of labor and the duties of capital, but in so doing they are inconsistent. Only individual laborers and capitalists are beings who can have rights and duties, if the application of ethical norms and principles is restricted to individuals. Groups cannot have rights and duties.

3. Critical Examination of the Traditional Classification

Two questions are crucial. First, is the assumption of the traditional classification necessary and valid? Are individual human beings the only direct moral agents? And secondly, is such a restriction forced upon us by the acceptance of the assumption? Must we refrain from applying ethical norms and principles to groups, associations, communities, and states? Is it really possible in this post-war era of

DEFINITION OF POLITICAL ETHICS

the modern world to hold the application of ethics within the narrow limits of relations between individuals? Is it not incumbent upon ethical thinkers today to make a new classification of the problems of applied ethics wide enough to comprise all of the various relationships of human life, however complicated these may be? These last two questions must unquestionably be answered most emphatically in the affirmative. Consequently the assumption and the implication of the traditional classification require further consideration.

If the discussion is restricted to the denizens of earth the assumption that individual human beings are the center of the total moral situation must be accepted. There would be no applied ethics if there were no beings with the intellectual capacity to discover and to apply ethical principles, and the only such beings dwelling on earth are highly civilized humans. There is no evidence that animals are capable of ethical reflection. Anthropologists doubt whether savages are, and admit that such morality as they possess is wholly rudimentary. Hence we must admit that the attainment of ethical knowledge is reserved for those peoples of the earth having a highly developed culture. And if its attainment is reserved to such peoples it follows that only such peoples are able to regulate their behavior by ethical principles. Hence the application of ethics is possible only in the highest type of human societies, and such societies are characterized by having in them uniquely developed individuals. In the final analysis we are forced to accept the assumption that individual human beings are the only direct moral agents.

The defects in the traditional classification are not due to the assumption upon which it rests but to the restriction of the application of ethics to individual agents. For individuals are members of and are affected by all kinds of associations and institutions which act for the welfare of their members. Hence ethical principles are and by right ought to be applicable to these groups. Even though such groups are not moral agents directly *they are indirectly*. To deny this, or to minimize its significance in classifying the problems of applied ethics, is to be misled by a tradition, and however much one should respect tradition he should never let it lead him into error.

In making the application of ethics revolve around individual moral agents we fail to do justice to the ethical problems involved in the relation of groups to each other. We are only able to bring in such problems indirectly as group relations affect individual welfare. But what we want to know is whether there is not a set of ethical standards that can be applied to group behavior. At present the regulation of groups in their relations to each other is left to municipal law. What we need to create, and are creating, is a body of moral opinion about the behavior of groups, and a set of ethical norms that will regulate such groups. To be sure there are already in existence ethical codes for some of the older professions, and there is now in the making a set of codes for various industries. These

DEFINITION OF POLITICAL ETHICS 11

codes are certainly not on a par with municipal law. They are at least quasi-ethical. This shows the necessity for a new classification of the problems of applied ethics.

Although there is municipal law to regulate relations between groups, some lawyers hold that there can be no law to regulate the relations of sovereign states to each other. Let us postpone consideration of the question of whether mankind will ever be able to create a body of international law that can really be enforced. It will here suffice to mention the fact that there are actual relations existing between sovereign states today about which ethical judgments are being made. The nations are being weighed in the balances and found wanting. A body of world opinion on international relations is in slow process of formation. Ethical principles are today being applied to the dealings of sovereign states with each other and with dependent peoples. But the traditional classification of the problems of applied ethics completely ignores this phase of the subject. Now a classification which subordinates the application of ethical principles to groups to their application to individuals, and which entirely omits their application to international relations cannot be regarded as an adequate classification today.

4. A RECONSTRUCTION OF THE TRADITIONAL CLASSIFICATION TO CORRECT THESE DEFECTS

Suppose we accept the application of ethics to the relations of individuals to each other as the first main division of Applied Ethics, and use the three basic questions of the traditional theory to subdivide this main division. This would give us:

I. The Application of Ethics to Individual Relations.
(Personal Ethics.)
- a. The Doctrine of Individual Rights.
- b. The Doctrine of Individual Duties.
- c. The Doctrine of Individual Virtues.

To this we may now add two other divisions, namely:

II. The Application of Ethics to Groups.
(Professional and Business Ethics.)
- a. The Doctrine of Group Rights.
  Rights of a physician, lawyer, etc.
  Rights of capital, of labor, etc.
- b. The Doctrine of Group Duties.
  Duties of physicians, lawyers, business men, etc.
- c. The Professional Virtues.
  Qualities of character for the professions.

III. The Application of Ethics to Relations between Peoples.
(Political Ethics.)
- a. The Doctrine of Rights of Peoples.
  1. Rights of progressive peoples.
  2. Rights of backward peoples.
  (See below, Chapters X and XI.)
- b. The Doctrine of Duties of Peoples.
  1. Duties of sovereign states to other sovereign states.
  2. Duties of sovereign states to dependent peoples.
- c. The Doctrine of National or Cultural Virtues.
  Unique contributions of each culture to world culture. (On the meaning of culture see below, Chapter IX.)

DEFINITION OF POLITICAL ETHICS 13

Note that we have subdivided each of these two main divisions by the same principle which was used in subdividing the first main division. Such a classification is much more adequate than the traditional classification, even though it necessarily involves considerable overlapping and must presently be corrected. A diagram may serve to clarify the three fields and their interrelations.

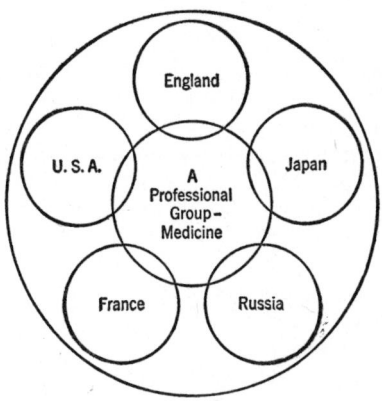

Let the large circle represent the human race as a whole with its millions of individuals. The large circles within it may then be used to represent separate major cultures. Smaller circles could be drawn within the circle designated England to represent colonies or commonwealths of the British Empire. A large circle cutting across the separate cultures and commonwealths may be used to represent a typical professional group. It is obvious that the application of ethical principles to individuals in their dealings with each other is not the whole of applied ethics. A man may be a citizen of the United States and have business or cultural relations with a man in Japan. Then personal ethics cuts across political ethics. The code of the American Medical Association should be essentially the same as the code of the Medical Association of any other country. Hence professional ethics cuts across political ethics. As the relations of individuals and groups reach wider ramifications the necessity for a wider application of ethical principles increases. Consequently, human beings will eventually develop an application of ethical principles to professional and economic groups and to separate cultures which will constitute a common applied ethics for all mankind. Obviously the principles applicable to all mankind will be fewer and far more general than those applicable to individuals within the same culture. In applying ethical principles and in passing ethical judgments it is incumbent upon the thinker to keep in mind the type of relation to which the application is made. Circumstances alter cases.

5. A Definition of Political Ethics. Delimitation of Its Subject Matter

Our classification restricts political ethics to the relations between cultural groups. This is a defect. Actually the subject matter of political ethics is much wider than relations between cultural groups.

We must include under political ethics the relations of the state to its individual members. What

DEFINITION OF POLITICAL ETHICS

do I owe the state? What does it do for me? Although these are questions an individual asks himself, they are none the less questions of political ethics. When a man formulates a conception of his relations to his own cultural group, he is within the general field of political ethics rather than that of personal ethics.

Moreover, the complicated relations between the state and separate groups within it are material for political ethics. Shall separate groups be permitted to make their own ethical codes? The modern state answers no. We have laws regulating all our industrial groups. Likewise we have laws regulating all our professional groups. But this is not entirely a legal matter, since wherever there is a statute law there is an ethical principle lurking near. The basic relations between the state and the groups operating under its laws are ethical. Since some of these groups overlap many states the ethical problem becomes extremely difficult. Few realize the importance of professional groups in modern life. Speaking of the sciences and the professions, Professor A. N. Whitehead says: "They constitute a clear-cut novelty within modern societies." And he especially stresses their international character and how they differ today from what they were in ancient times. "In the earlier centuries the professional influence, as a general sociological fact, was mainly a welter of bygone flashes of intelligence relapsing into customary procedures. It represented the continual lapse of intellect into instinct. But the culmination of science completely inverted the rôles of custom and intelligence in the older professions. By this inversion professional institutions have acquired an international life. Each such institution practices within its own nation, but its sources of life are world-wide. Thus loyalties stretch beyond sovereign states. Perhaps the most important function of these institutions is the supervision of standards of individual professional competence and of professional practice. For this purpose there is a complex interweaving of universities and more specialized institutions." [6] Concurring fully in what Dr. Whitehead says, we must especially emphasize the importance of the application of ethical principles to the relation of states to professional groups.

And yet the relationships that are especially troublesome are those between one state and another, since many of the existing states are backward in their cultural development. How should a progressive state treat a backward people? Some backward peoples are politically dependent on a progressive state. Others are relatively free and sovereign powers. How are we to determine backwardness and progressiveness? What relations between sovereign states are ethical, and what relations between sovereign states and backward peoples are ethical? These are all burning questions of political ethics. This wide scope of political ethics may

[6] From A. N. Whitehead: *Adventures of Ideas*, pp. 79 and 77, reprinted by permission of The Macmillan Company, Publishers.

DEFINITION OF POLITICAL ETHICS

be summarized in another diagram which is intended to correct the first.

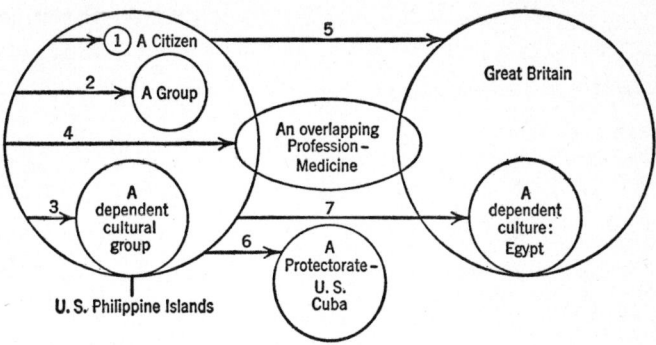

The numbered arrows indicate various kinds of relations which form the subject matter of political ethics. These are: (1) The relations between a sovereign state and its individual members or citizens. (2) The relations between a sovereign state and its internal groups, that is, those groups whose activities fall entirely within that state. (3) The relations between a sovereign state and minor cultural groups under its jurisdiction. (4) The relations between a sovereign state and overlapping groups, that is, those whose activities overlap other sovereign states besides the one in which they have their home base. (5) The relations between sovereign states. (6) The relations of sovereign states to their protectorates. (7) The relation of the people of one sovereign state to a cultural group wholly dependent upon another sovereign state.

Each of these kinds of relations is highly complicated, involving many concrete or actual relations, numerous examples of which will occur to the reader. And it should be especially noted that the seven types of relations indicated in the diagram are not exhaustive, and that some of them would differ considerably if they were thought of in the reverse direction from that indicated by the arrows. Think of the relation of a sovereign state to a citizen of another sovereign state, or of the relation of a sovereign state to a business corporation organized and operating under the laws of another sovereign state. Think, too, of the relation of the Filipino people to the United States when viewed from their angle. Obviously no diagram is adequate to express all of these details. It follows that the subject matter of political ethics is enormously complex and involved. Hence we cannot expect to do more than scratch the surface of this complexity. Nevertheless we will at least try to do that. It is a widely accepted principle that morality tends to sink to a lower level as we pass from the behavior of individuals to the activities of wider and wider groups. It is a well known fact that an infuriated mob of human beings will occasionally commit a crime, the mere thought of doing which would horrify most of the individuals in the mob. There is truth in this idea and yet it is not wholly true. Infuriated individuals often run amuck, and it may be doubted whether the quality of fury in such individuals differs from that moving a mob. It is better

DEFINITION OF POLITICAL ETHICS

to say that the degree to which an ethical principle is applicable varies with the type of relation to which it is applied, and that the number of ethical concepts applicable to individuals is much larger than the number applicable to relations between peoples. This fact must be kept continually in mind, and we will discuss it more at length in Chapter VIII.

We must begin by laying down a philosophical theory of what the state is. Political ethics not only presupposes theoretical ethics, but also theoretical political philosophy. To deal adequately with the complicated problems in any systematic way means to adopt some position on the philosophical question: *What is the state?*

What to Read

On the relation between the morality of civilized peoples and that of savages, see Dewey and Tufts: *Ethics* (Revised Edition) chapters I-V, and the article entitled *Ethics (Rudimentary)* by R. R. Marett in Hastings' *Encyclopedia of Religion and Ethics,* Vol. V, pp. 426 ff.

On the meaning of Applied Ethics see W. M. Urban: *Fundamentals of Ethics,* Chapter IX, and C. F. Taeusch: *Professional and Business Ethics,* Chapter III. The *Code of Medical Ethics* is obtainable from the Secretary of the American Medical Association, and the *Canons of Legal and Judicial Ethics* is obtainable from the Secretary of the American Bar Association. Rotary International and other service clubs, and the Chamber of Commerce of the United States have formulated codes of business ethics. See also: *The Ethics of the Teaching Profession*—a bulletin issued by the National Education Association; N. A. Crawford: *The Ethics of Journalism;* and E. C. Heermance: *Codes of Ethics* (contains 198 codes of all professions and occupations). The N. R. A. codes are obtainable from the Government Printing Office, and are printed separately for each industry. See also: *Labor and the New Deal* by Emannuel Stein, Carl Raushenbush, and Lewis MacDonald; and Raymond Moley's article entitled: *The Meaning of the N. R. A.* in the volume entitled *The Liberal Way,* pp. 241-250. The book by Professor Taeusch cited above gives one interpretation of business ethics. Three other viewpoints are presented in Dean E. Lord's *Fundamentals of Business Ethics;* Harry F. Ward's *Our Economic Morality;* and R. C. Cabot's *Adventures on the Borderland of Ethics.*

See also Bruno Burn: *Codes, Cartels, National Planning; Current Economic Policies,* a source book by various authors; Ford P. Hall: *Government and Business;* and James M. Lee: *Business Ethics.*

A pre-war classic dealing with political relations is T. H. Green: *Principles of Political Obligation.* Some important post-war books are: B. Bosanquet: *Social and International Ideals;* C. Deslie Burns: *The Morality of Nations;* George E. G. Catlin: *A Study of the Principles of Politics,* pp. 39-56; Francis W. Coker: *Recent Political Thought;* John Dewey: *The Public and Its Problems;* Hans Driesch: *Ethical Principles in Theory and Practice,* pp. 117-186; W. Y. Elliott: *The Pragmatic Revolt in Politics,* Parts III-V; Seba Eldridge: *The New Citizenship;* M. P. Follett: *The New State;* W. E. Hocking: *The Spirit of World Politics;* H. J. Laski: *The Grammar of Politics;* Walter Lippmann: *The Method of Freedom;* William MacDougall: *Ethics and Some Modern World Problems;* Charles E. Merriam: *New Aspects of Politics;* Reinhold Niebuhr:

Moral Man and Immoral Society; M. C. Otto: *Things and Ideals;* Bertrand Russell: *Political Ideals;* Norman Wilde: *The Ethical Basis of the State;* W. W. Willoughby: *The Ethical Basis of Political Authority.*

CHAPTER II

WHY THERE ARE STATES

1. THE CHILD'S CONCEPTION OF THE STATE

Let us approach a definition of the state through a study of its relation to the individual, since this relationship is the one to which ethical principles most certainly apply. Whether the actions of a state directed towards other peoples fall within the scope of political ethics may be and has been denied, but no one can question the ethical significance of the relation of a state to its own citizens.

The mature and reflective individual knows his own state to be the source of most of the values he enjoys, as well as the chief agency of restraint and check upon many of the actions he considers doing. To him his own state is the most omnipresent of the realities with which he deals in his practical everyday life. But he learns this from experience. There is no innate idea of the state. It makes us what we are before we even know what it is.

Think back in your own experience to the days of your childhood and you will find that you have no memory of having had then any conception of the state as a whole. You can remember experiencing your family relationships. You can remember

WHY THERE ARE STATES

going to school and to church and participating in community life. But you cannot recall ever having had any definite idea of that larger and more omnipresent reality, which, from the moment of your birth, was the major influence in shaping you, in making you what you are.

Even those young people who have studied civics and American history in high school remain relatively provincial. The only part of the state they really know is their local community. They have a vague idea of its being a part of a larger whole, but their activities and thoughts are largely confined within the restricted region of some definite neighborhood, and they usually and normally develop a genuine attachment for their own community. This provincialism of youth is the indispensable condition of the development of genuine love of country. Think of Sir Walter Scott's noble lines:

> Breathes there a man with soul so dead
> Who never to himself has said,
> This is my own, my native land?

Such love of country is the product of provincialism. True patriotism is rooted back in love of native environs, in attachment to some definite neighborhood. Professor Josiah Royce recognized this in his *Philosophy of Loyalty* and in his *Race Questions and Other American Problems,* where he especially stressed the need of developing what he called a wise provincialism in American life as the basis for a love of country.

Patriotism is an emotion which ordinarily arises during those early years of childhood in which the individual immerses himself in the life of a local community. Such a local community is almost all that the state is to uneducated and simple-minded people throughout their lives. One of the real dangers in the development of rapid facilities for transportation and communication is the tendency toward the inhibition of the formation of a healthy sentiment for local community life. The increase of criminality among young people may be partly due to this fact. It is important that children should get their first insight into what the state is by participating in the life of a relatively small local community, and our modern elementary and secondary schools are rendering a great service in giving American children this insight. The aim of many educators is to make their school a model community.

When youth widens its outlook and deepens its contacts this provincialism perforce gradually disappears. And it should, since the narrowness and exclusiveness of provincialism are real evils. Wisely led young people discover that they share the life of the "Great Community" constituted by the entire history, growth and expansion, and present creative activities of millions of human beings whose aims and interests reflect a common communal life. Love of local community is then extended to this more inclusive and far richer life. The youth becomes conscious of a deep obligation to the great host of the dead who created and transmitted this culture to his generation, and of an equally deep obligation to enrich it a little more and pass it on to posterity. This is the actual living experience of the state as it should be born anew in each youth of every generation.

2. Stages in the Development of Social Consciousness

Let us illustrate, with a few lines from one of America's greatest poets, the close relation that exists between love of local community, true patriotism, and humanitarianism. Walt Whitman's poems prove that he knew full well that these are identical in their essence and that taken together they constitute a well-rounded and completely developed social consciousness. Born and reared in Brooklyn, he expresses the influence of the great metropolis upon him in these vibrant lines:

Fear not—submit to no models but your own, O City!
Behold me—incarnate me as I have incarnated you!
I have rejected nothing you offered me—whom you adopted
    I have adopted,
Good or bad I never question you—I love all—I do not
    condemn anything
I chant and celebrate all that is yours.

And again this love of his own city is beautifully expressed in *Manhatta,* the title of which he explains in the opening lines:

I was asking for something specific and perfect for my city,
Whereupon lo, upsprang the aboriginal name.

and which ends exultingly:

A million people—manners free and superb—open voices—
    hospitality—the most courageous and friendly
    young men,
City of hurried and sparkling waters! city of spires and
    masts!
City nested in bays! my city!

Yet even more than his city Walt Whitman loved "these States," and no American poet has better formulated in words the experience of the state as all young people should experience it. In his *Song of the Redwood-Tree* he sings of the "hidden national will" which is "conceal'd but ever alert." And in his poem entitled *For You, O Democracy*, he conceives of the whole nation being held together by those same bonds of comradeship which he found in the city.

Come, I will make the continent indissoluble,
I will make the most splendid race the sun ever shone upon,
I will make divine magnetic lands,
    With the love of comrades,
        With the life-long love of comrades.

I will plant companionship thick as trees along the rivers of
    America and along the shores of the great lakes, and
    all over the prairies,
I will make inseparable cities with their arms about each
    other's necks,
    By the love of comrades,
        By the manly love of comrades.

For you these from me, O Democracy, to serve you, ma
 femme!
For you, for you I am trilling these songs.

Yes, Walt Whitman knew what the state is because he experienced its throbbing, pulsating life, first in the great city of his birth, then on his "journeys through the States," and then on the battlefields and in the hospitals as an angel of mercy to the soldiers of both the North and the South who bled even unto death that "these States" might become truly indissoluble. But we know that this did not make him cease to love all mankind. For in the matchless lines of his *Passage to India* this great souled and loyal American poet also expressed his sense of oneness with all races, all cultures, all peoples. Here are six prophetic lines that give the central theme:

Lo, soul! seest thou not God's purpose from the first?
The earth to be spann'd, connected by net-work
The people to become brothers and sisters,
The races, neighbors, to marry and be given in marriage,
The oceans to be cross'd, the distant brought near,
The lands to be welded together.

And elsewhere he writes:

Flaunt out, O sea, your separate flags of nations!
Flaunt out visible as ever the various ship-signals!
But do you reserve especially for yourself and for the soul
 of man one flag above all the rest,

A spiritual woven signal for all nations, . . .
A pennant universal, subtly waving all time, o'er all brave
    sailors,
All seas, all ships.

The gradual development of social consciousness, until it flowers in perfection in great souls like Walt Whitman, is perfectly natural. Such geniuses apparently never feel any conflict between love of local community, love of country, and love of all mankind, since all of these sentiments are harmoniously blended to form their total social consciousness. In a valuable recent book, giving the results of painstaking research, Mr. H. E. Englebrecht traces the development of the social consciousness of the great German philosopher, Johann Gottlieb Fichte, who is especially important to us because of his direct influence upon Thomas Carlyle and his indirect influence upon Ralph Waldo Emerson. Mr. Englebrecht shows how Fichte passed from an affection for his local environs (*Heimatsliebe*) to a final synthesis of patriotism and cosmopolitanism, and he explains how various interpreters of this great German thinker have been misled by taking one or the other of these attitudes as exclusive of the other, some treating him as a narrow nationalist and others as a great humanitarian. As a matter of fact his social consciousness was so fully and so harmoniously developed that there was no essential conflict between these sentiments.[1]

[1] See H. E. Englebrecht: *Johann Gottlieb Fichte.* See the quotation from Fichte below, pp. 198 f.

WHY THERE ARE STATES

As our brief study of Walt Whitman and this bare reference to Fichte indicate, there are a number of different stages in the evolution of social consciousness. These are graphically portrayed in the following table:

Table Showing the Chief Levels of Social Consciousness

Basic Human Sentiment	Social Group or Institution
Filial love	Family or Kinship Group
Love of local environs	Neighborhood, City
Love of native customs (Sectionalism, Provincialism)	A section or Province
Love of country (Patriotism)	The State or Nation
Love of one's language and culture	English-speaking people Christian people
Love of all mankind (Humanitarianism, Cosmopolitanism)	Humanity as a whole

Commoner natures are often incapable of developing fully the sentiments for the wider groups. They are even likely to think that loyalty to some lesser group demands suspicion, intolerance, hostility towards and even hatred of other groups. Most forms of criminality are due to a perverted social consciousness, as is proven by the fact that gangsters and brigands band together in a loyalty unto death in their attacks on larger social groups. On the other hand, what makes some men saints and sages is that they learn how to bring all of these sentiments into harmony by subordinating them to something like Spinoza's consuming passion, which he called the intellectual love of God. Spinoza was certainly right in thinking that our social sentiments are mutually compatible, or, at least, that they can be made so by being brought under the control of and merged with reason. Practically all the great sages and saints of the world testify to this eternal truth. Confucius, Buddha, Lao Tze, Socrates, and Jesus all taught their followers to love all mankind as well as their own people.

Unfortunately many individuals never develop anything like a complete and harmonious social consciousness, but remain throughout life relatively provincial and deeply prejudiced against strangers and their customs. Hence they develop a narrow type of patriotism, and fail to discover that genuine love of country is compatible with compassion for all fellow creatures. Some even consider the state to be a great evil because of the restraint it places upon them in their efforts to satisfy their animal desires. To others it appears as a device of wicked wise men to exploit good ignorant men, while still others regard it as but a half-way stage to the development of that full solidarity of all mankind in which separate states will give way to a genuine internationalism. What, then, is the state? What is it from the standpoint of the reflecting individual? Is it really what we want to preserve, or is it something we should make every effort to destroy?

3. Hobbes and Rousseau Contrasted

We might get help in answering these questions by turning to some of the great classical philosophers. For many of them have given deep consideration to the problem of the nature of the state. In the *Republic,* the greatest of the works of Plato, we find a sketch of an ideal state, which has been an unending source of inspiration to other thinkers. He argued that the state is the individual "writ large" or in capital letters. Ideally it is a living organism with a class of philosophers imposing a rule of reason on the class of courageous guardians, as well as that of temperate tradesmen and workingmen, and where each of these groups is creating justice by attending to its own business. No such state has ever existed and it is a safe prophecy that none ever will. Of course Plato knew this for he makes Socrates say: "You must not insist on my proving that the actual state will in every respect coincide with the ideal: if we are only able to discover how a city may be governed nearly as we proposed, you will . . . be contented. I am sure that I should be contented—will not you?" [2]

Campanella revived Plato's conception in his famous *City of the Sun* where wise priests were to rule instead of philosophers. Francis Bacon placed scientists at the head of his ideal state as portrayed in the fragment entitled *The New Atlantis.* All these are descriptions of the perfect state that can never be.

Certain other philosophers have been more realistic. They have attempted to tell what the state is which actually exists. Aristotle's conception,

[2] Plato: *Republic,* V, p. 473 (Jowett's translation).

based upon the small city-state of the ancient world, and Spinoza's view of the state as essentially the power of a culture to preserve itself, are examples of such realistic conceptions. But it will be especially enlightening for us to consider the social contract theories of Thomas Hobbes and of Jean Jacques Rousseau, since these theories stand in rather sharp contrast but contain a common idea.

The common idea in the theories of Hobbes and Rousseau is that the state exists because men desire it as a means of making their earthly existence tolerable. They think man made the state, and that man would rather be under the authority and power of the state than to live in the kind of a world he would have to endure if there were no state. This idea is profound and true. The state is civilized man's instrument for lessening the evils and for enhancing and enriching the values of his existence. We shall return to this idea presently.

Hobbes conceived of a "state of nature" in which men were perpetually fighting each other. He vividly describes this original condition of mankind as a war of all against all—*bellum omnium contra omnes*. Such a condition of unending strife made each individual's life "poor, nasty, brutish, and short." Naturally nobody liked this way of existing. So men formed a rational compact in which each agreed to stop fighting his fellows and surrendered a part of his power to a sovereign authority who made everybody keep the agreement. Thus Hobbes thought that the state was created by men to keep down the evils that arise from each one fighting everyone else to preserve his own life. In the state of nature the law of self-preservation: Every man for himself and the devil take the hindermost, prevailed. Under the state the first law of nature and of reason was "Seek peace and preserve it." And Hobbes thought the best state was one in which the power was concentrated in one absolute monarch, who was justified in giving vogue to the fiction of the divine right of kings. For did this fiction not strengthen his authority and thereby augment his power? Of course, the trouble with Hobbes' theory is that the idea of a state of nature, as well as that of an actual social contract being the basis of the state, are also both fictions, but this weakness should not blind us to the profound truth in his theory.

Rousseau did not pretend to give a precise description of the state of nature, although he thought it was a condition in which all men were free. He thought that the state enslaves both rulers and subjects. He admitted that he could not explain why men gave up a condition of freedom for one of slavery, or how the change from one condition to the other took place. But he thought he could tell what makes the change legitimate. In his own words at the opening of his famous *Social Contract*: "Man is born free, and everywhere he is in chains. One thinks himself the master of others, who does not fail to be more of a slave than they. How did this change take place? I do not know? What can render it legitimate? I think I can tell." Briefly stated, Rousseau's view is that man prefers to be in the chains which living in the state involves to suffering the evils of a life lived in perpetual conflict with the forces of nature. So men created organized society to minimize the struggle for existence. It was the evils of the quest for subsistence that Rousseau made the basis for the state. Men united spontaneously that they might gain a greater control over the forces of nature and thereby enrich culture.

Hobbes said the state was formed to keep men from fighting each other. Rousseau said it resulted from a common will or purpose to make life better by a coöperative mastery of the evils of nature. Both thinkers said that man preferred the state to the evils he would have had to suffer in a world of social anarchy. And they were both right. Man wants the state and needs it and wills it as the best way to contend with the evils of existence and to realize the higher cultural values. This is the best approach to an understanding of the real function of the state in human life.

4. THREE KINDS OF EVILS AGAINST WHICH MAN CONTENDS

The state evolved as an instrument further to surmount the evils of the struggle for existence and the defects of those forms of social organization which preceded it. There never was what Hobbes called "the state of nature" and what Rousseau called the state of complete freedom. Modern anthropology has made us fully cognizant of the fact that elementary forms of human life are always highly organized by unwritten codes, and that the historical state develops on the basis of this earlier tribal life. But unlike Topsy in *Uncle Tom's Cabin*, it did not just grow. It was produced by civilized peoples endeavoring to mitigate the evils of their manner of living. Professor Wilde rightly says: "We do not speak of the African or Australian native peoples as constituting states, or of the states of the Homeric age, or of early Indian groups, although these people exercised most of the powers now embodied in the modern state. Indeed the powers of the early tribe were more rather than fewer, and its authority greater rather than less; life, death, property, marriage, and religion being absolutely in the hands of the tribal group. Every essential feature of his life was determined for the individual: he was born, he lived, he died as sacred custom prescribed. There was no destructive individualism in those beginnings of social life, but the whole was instinctively, unquestionedly the presupposition of the parts. And it is in these very characteristics that we get the essential distinction in principle between the early tribal organization and the state; the former is based upon custom and exhibits little specialization of function, the latter is the expression of reflection and therefore shows increasing specialization and delimitation of powers. Instead of tradition, without historic origin and principle of growth, we have laws of known history and changing character; and in place of the all-embracing authority of the elders of the tribe, we have the fixed constitution and the definite prescription of political rights. Reflection has supervened upon instinct and, while the concentrated absolutism of the tribe may be repeated in some forms of the state, it is done consciously and of purpose and with recognition of the situation involved. Government as a special function has come into existence and political organization has been distinguished, if not separated, from the religious and economic. In this sense the state is a product of civilization rather than of nature, an association or an institution rather than an unconscious growth." [3]

Nevertheless there is an element of truth in Rousseau's contention that the state enslaves both rulers and subjects. For new evils came with the state. From the standpoint of an individual moral agent, striving to attain the fullest possible development of all of his specifically human capacities, there are at least three chief types of evils in modern organized society.

(1) *The Clash of Ideals.*—Such an individual will inevitably find a conflict between what he wants to make out of himself and what the group or groups to which he belongs wish to make out of him. He is not at first conscious of this conflict because his own personal ideal is merely latent in him and only gradually becomes definite as his experiences widen

---

[3] Norman Wilde: *The Ethical Basis of the State* (Princeton University Press), p. 13 f.

and his self grows. But sooner or later he awakens to the fact that there is an inevitable *clash of ideals* in whatever social order he lives. He finds that there are forces trying to mold him in definite directions and that some of these directions are not in accordance with his own idea of what he wants to be. For every individual is unique and group life is relatively standardized. Each person is a vital energizing forward-pushing self and such selves are bound to come into conflict with the goals that are set for them by society. They yearn to seek for other goals. Hence the clash of ideals is inevitable, unavoidable, rooted in the very nature of human vitality. Yet how could a man even form an ideal without some acquaintance with the rich cultural inheritance of some great people? How could he be an artist, if there were no art, or a scientist, if there were no science, or a rabbi, priest, or clergyman, if there were no religion, or a business man, if there were no trade? And how could there be these cultural values, if there were no state? So we must conclude that the evils due to the clash of ideals is not sufficient to justify an attitude of hostility to the state. It is better to have the ideals and the clash than it is not to have the ideals at all. So man needs the state to conserve the cultural values he himself helps to create, and to make it possible for him to form ideals and to seek objectives that will enrich his own life.

(2) *The Competitive Nature of Economic Value.*—Under the aegis of the modern state man-

kind has accumulated the greatest store of economic goods and of capital which the world has ever known. There was nothing to compare with it in even the greatest states of the Ancient World. All the treasures of ancient Rome, India, China, Egypt, and Babylonia combined would not begin to equal the amassed wealth in goods and capital of the British Commonwealth of Nations. But earth's population has also enormously increased. And the standard of living has greatly changed for the more fortunate members of the human race. So there is not yet, and probably never will be, enough goods and capital to supply every single individual's needs for such values. Consequently, there are the evils due to the inability of any modern state to make a just distribution of these competitive values. And yet we must remember that without the state these goods would not exist in the quantities available today. And again, man must prefer to have the goods with the evils of unjust distribution to not having the goods at all. Hence this kind of evil does not justify an anarchial society. Men need the state to make possible the accumulation and equitable distribution of economic values.

(3) *The Fixity of Institutions.* — From the standpoint of a growing individual the institutions through which he must seek the enrichment of his life are too rigid. And the older a state is the more hoary with age are its institutions, and the more fixed and rigid they become. Classes develop and fight for their own rights and prerogatives. Old

WHY THERE ARE STATES

men, whose minds have become senile, sit in high places and bar the way to younger and more virile leaders. Science devises ways to prolong life until the average age reaches fifty years or more, and this makes the lot of youth all the harder. Institutions resist change. They function according to fixed grooves of procedure. He who seeks the values they have to offer must work under all sorts of handicaps, and oftentimes his life gets warped in the process. There seems to be no way in which to get rid of the institutionalized evils. The money-changers will forever be defiling the temple. And yet without the state there would be no institutions through which the individual could realize himself. The evils in institutions do not justify the destruction of the state.

5. How to Deal With These Evils

Much popular and some technical political philosophy is based upon a false assumption of how these evils should be met. That assumption is that a state should be created which would eliminate all three kinds of evils *in toto*. Criminals and rebels attack the actually existing social order because they are unable to satisfy their needs in it. The criminal takes whatever he can get. The rebel tries to set up a social order from which the evils are all eradicated, but the assumption that this is possible is a false assumption.

It cannot be emphasized too much that all three of the kinds of evils expounded above are inherent in any social order whatsoever. If there are many unique individuals their ideals of what they want to make of themselves will clash with the group's ideals of what they want to make out of their members. Competitive values are by their very nature restricted to the use of those who actually do use them. They do not grow by being shared as do the cultural values. Institutions will stay relatively fixed. It is essential to their continuance that they should have greater stability than the individuals who use them in realizing themselves. Hence all three types of evils are inherent in any social order, and it is a mistake to think that some other than the actually existing state would succeed in destroying these evils.

This has been well expressed by a contribution in the Contributor's Column of the *Atlantic Monthly* [4] in which the author contrasts the method an individual has to use to get his share of economic goods under a Democracy with that required in Russia under the Soviet system. The technique of getting on differs in the two systems, and the one is symbolically designated *horse trading* and the other *wangling*. Horse trading is a process of "exchanging things of less value for things of more value," and it operates between individuals in those states characterized as capitalistic. Wangling "is a method of getting some article, or the use of some article, or the enjoyment of some power or privilege out of somebody who does not himself own it, and who is

[4] See Vol. 152, pp. 635 ff.

WHY THERE ARE STATES 41

not supposed to exchange or grant or allocate it for his own benefit, and who is administering it as a trustee for its real owner, the community at large." The widespread use of wangling in those states and groups where authority takes the place of property rights shows that we do not get rid of the evils inherent in the nature of competitive values by destroying one social order and setting up another. We merely change the technique of getting on. Shrewd people quit their horse trading tactics and substitute the technique of wangling.

Instead of trying to eliminate these three kinds of evils let us recognize that they are inherent in the very nature of human life. Let us agree with Hobbes that there will always be a certain amount of conflict among people over the values of life. Let us admit Rousseau's contention that man must always struggle with the forces of nature. Let us never forget that the maintenance of civilization and the conservation and enhancement of the higher cultural values is an endless task. Let us remember that as long as men dwell on the earth they will be forced to fight against disease, pestilence, tempests, hurricanes, in short against all the brute forces of the natural environment which happens to form their habitat. And let us also remember that men will always have to fight against greed, avarice, lust, in short, against all the perversions to which human flesh is subject. We may as well make the most of the fact that no state can possibly eliminate all of these evils. But how can we make the most of such an untoward fact?

The answer is by building the kind of a social order which will grow and adjust itself in such a way as to keep all three kinds of evils in constant check. We can never build a Utopia. No absolutely perfect state will ever exist on earth. Every actual state will have all three kinds of evils in it. The best state will be that one which is so flexible in its organization, and so nicely balanced in its structure, that it will always serve as a check on every kind of evil. Let us attempt to set up such an ideal state, realizing that its perfection cannot consist in the exclusion of all evils from its life but in its ability to keep every kind of evil under constant check. A Utopia would be like a university made up of Phi Beta Kappa students, intolerable both to students and teachers. Every actual state should and will contain an almost infinite variety of individuals all of whom will contribute to the enrichment of its culture.

What to Read

Thomas Hobbes: *Leviathan,* and J. J. Rousseau: *The Social Contract* are the classic works on the social contract theory of the state. Selections from both works are available in D. S. Robinson: *Anthology of Modern Philosophy,* as are also selections from Spinoza, Fichte, and Hegel on political philosophy. The best statement of the Hegelian theory of the state is B. Bosanquet's *Philosophical Theory of the State.* L. T. Hobhouse: *The Metaphysical Theory of*

WHY THERE ARE STATES

the State gives a thorough critique of the Hegelian political philosophy.

There are many recent works on the state, some of the most valuable of which are the following: Felix Adler: *An Ethical Philosophy of Life,* pp. 305-324; S. Parkes Cadman: *Christianity and the State,* Lect. III-V; F. W. Coker: *Organismic Theories of the State;* S. H. M. Chang: *The Marxian Theory of the State;* John Dewey: *The Public and its Problems,* Ch. II; W. E. Hocking: *Man and the State;* C. E. M. Joad: *Modern Political Theory;* H. Krabbe: *The Modern Idea of the State,* translated by George H. Sabine and Walter J. Shepard (the long translators' introduction is especially enlightening); H. J. Laski: *Grammar of Politics,* Chs. I-II; R. M. MacIver: *The Modern State,* Introduction and Book IV; Leonidas Pitamic: *A Treatise on the State,* Pt. I; J. H. Randall: *The Making of the Modern Mind;* J. H. Tufts: *The Real Business of Living,* Part I.

In his *The Origin of the State,* R. H. Lowie explains how the state arose out of tribal organization. See also the references given in the concluding paragraph of the reading list at the end of Chapter I.

CHAPTER III

THE POSTULATES OF AN IDEAL STATE

1. Explanation of Terminology

Since the state arises to meet the three kinds of evils described in the preceding chapter let us endeavor to define an ideal state that would be sufficiently well organized to constitute a perpetual check on these evils. A preliminary explanation of terminology will clarify the problem.

We propose to restrict the use of the term *Utopia* to those ideal states from which all evils have been abstracted, and which in consequence are incapable of actualization. This restriction is in accordance with the original meaning of the word, which became a common designation of an ideal state as a result of Sir Thomas More's use of it as the title of his book describing such a state. The word is of Greek derivation, and its literal meaning is "not a place." A Utopia is a pure fiction. No Utopia can become real. Yet an ideal state may be so defined that it is capable of being actualized. Such a state must be one based on the assumption that the evils described above are ineradicable, and which will aim to check these evils instead of removing them entirely. It will be perfect only in the sense that it is a flexible and an adaptable instrument capable of meeting new situations, perfect as a knife or a machine may be said to be perfect, perfect because efficient in providing a constant check on the evils of any organized community. It is in this sense that we propose to use the term *ideal state*.

In setting up such a realizable ideal state Professor W. E. Hocking has suggested definite *postulates* to meet each type of evil discussed at the end of Chapter II. The term *postulate* is now generally used as a name for any highly general principle that is assumed rather than demonstrated, and yet which is not self-evident or axiomatic. Originally it was used to designate certain non-axiomatic and yet indemonstrable principles in mathematics. Due to the influence of Immanuel Kant, this term has come to be widely used by philosophers to refer to the fundamental ethical principles which are necessary to constitute a moral universe, but which cannot be demonstrated as true in the same way in which scientific laws can be demonstrated. All that can be done is to show that they are necessary to the constitution of a moral universe. Kant's three famous postulates of morality, which he regarded as corollaries of his categorical imperative (see above, p. 6), were *the existence of God, the freedom of the human will,* and *immortality*. Today many thinkers would substitute the belief in the continued progress of the human race for Kant's postulate of immortality, but they would treat this belief as a postulate as Kant defined that term.

Using the term postulate in this Kantian sense, Professor Hocking sets up certain basic moral principles that could be the basis of an actual state which would correct the evils already described. These principles constitute a set of postulates of an ideal state. Any state which incorporated them actually would be a constant check on the three evils. In *Human Nature and Its Remaking* (Part V) Professor Hocking has stated his set of postulates very clearly, and he has also there worked out the mechanism by which each of the first two postulates serves as a check on each of the first two evils. However, he names the first postulate only and I have suggested names for the other three. Moreover, he seems to me to have confused somewhat his statement of the mechanism of the first two postulates, by including in it certain actualizations of this mechanism here in the United States. I am proposing to correct this defect by stating each mechanism purely ideally, and by briefly indicating a mechanism to accompany the last two postulates, which form a pair to correct the third evil. Note that for the time being we are merely setting up an ideal state without implying that any actually existing state does in any way comply with the requirements of this set of postulates. The degree to which various actual states incorporate these ideal principles, and the mechanisms essential to their effective functioning, is reserved for later consideration.

2. The Postulate of Identical Ideals

We could correct the evils that come from the clash of ideals if we had a social order which embodied the principle: *"What others wish me to be must be identical with what I myself wish to be"* Hocking. Or we might word this postulate as follows: *What the state aims to make out of each of its citizens must be identical with what each citizen wants to make out of himself.* This same principle seems to be implied in John Dewey's famous statement, epitomizing his educational philosophy, "What the best and wisest parent wants for his own child, that must the community want for all of its children." [1] Is it possible to secure such an identity of ideals?

It might be objected that no individual, not even the wisest, really knows what he wants to make out of himself, or out of his children, if he is a parent. Knowing what one wants is no simple matter. We may know that we have certain momentary desires that crave immediate satisfaction, but knowing what one really wants to make out of oneself or one's children is undoubtedly extremely difficult. But if we can assume that there is a latent idea of good in each human being, a unique moral deposit that guides him in the quest for full self-development, then it should be possible in the course of time for each youth in a state to formulate for himself an ideal of what he wants to become. And

[1] John Dewey: *School and Society,* p. 19. (Univ. of Chicago Press)

unless we assume some such original moral deposit ethics is reduced to a division of biology. It is really implicit in the assumption that individuals are the only direct moral agents.

Other critics might object that the state is incapable of forming a conscious ideal of what it wants to make out of its citizens. It was probably because of this objection that Professor Hocking worded this postulate: "What others wish me to be," instead of: "What the state aims to make out of each of its citizens." Yet states, functioning through their leaders, actually do formulate definite ideals of what they want to make out of their citizens. Whether they are capable of doing this or not, they presume to do it. Hence our postulate explicitly takes account of the fact that states are trying to shape the ideals of young people, and sets up as the ideal *par excellence* that they should want to make out of them what they earnestly desire to make out of themselves. So the postulate cannot be ruled out as impossible.

Granted that this first postulate is abstractly within the realm of possibility, what specific arrangements in a social order are needed to make it concretely possible, that is, to make it actually realizable in practice? In answering this question let us prescribe certain requirements that must be met by actual states, if the postulate of identical ideals is to be realized.

There must be within each state a mixture of interested and of disinterested ideals, so that each youth may come into contact with the objective materials for bringing to full expression the germ or latent idea of good in his own mind. Naturally his parents and other "well wishers" will want him to develop along some definite line. Let us call all such ideals *interested,* since those formulating them for a youth have some special interest in what that youth is to become. But there should also be in every state a number of professional "recommenders" of ideals, persons having no special interest in a particular youth's development, but who do believe strongly in that separate field of activity which they represent. Let us call the ideals of such recommenders *disinterested ideals.* Now each youth, coming in close contact with the interested ideals of his well wishers and with the disinterested ideals of the recommenders, and guided by his own latent idea of what good is, will form a fairly definite ideal of what he wants to make out of himself.

The key to an understanding of the process by which the individual shapes his own ideal by utilizing this objective material is to be found in an analysis of the sentiment of admiration. Professor Hocking gives us such an analysis under the name the *anatomy of admiration.* He calls this the missing link in the logic by which we prove that the postulate of identical ideals can be complied with in an actual society. From the standpoint of a particular youth, one can formulate the first postulate like this: What I admire in others I wish for myself. Continuing in Professor Hocking's own words: "It is logically impossible for him to detach his thought of himself from his thought of others; because in every instance, including his own, consciousness shows him at once the individual and the *type*. In every human event, he is perceiving *man*. But this general principle, that what one admires one admires universally, applies also to the admirations of others: they cannot emancipate their admirations from their experience. Hence admiration is held within the scope of the possible; and it tends to be true of all fundamental values, that *What others admire, I admire*. The connection with our postulate is therewith complete. What others would admire in me tends to agree with what I actually admire in them: and what I admire in them I must admire (and wish for) in myself: hence, what they would admire in me, I must wish for in myself." [2] Thus the synthesis of a youth's latent idea of good with the interested and disinterested ideals supplied to him by well wishers and by recommenders, which is achieved through the functioning of the sentiment of admiration, does make the realization of the postulate of identical ideals concretely possible.

Now an ideal state, so far as the evils resulting from the conflict of ideals are concerned, would be one in which each youth's sentiment of admiration could function properly. It would be one in which

[2] W. E. Hocking: *Human Nature and Its Remaking*, 2nd ed., p. 221. Yale University Press. The terms "well wishers," "recommenders," and "interested and disinterested ideals" are borrowed from Professor Hocking.

POSTULATES OF AN IDEAL STATE 51

there were numerous and various recommenders, and it would be one in which the rulers encouraged the formation of individual ideals and gave the citizens the opportunity to realize these in their own lives. Such a state would be wholly interested in making the objective conditions under which its citizens lived such as would encourage the development of all the talent latent in these citizens.

3. THE POSTULATE OF THE TRANSFORMATION OF COMPETITIVE INTO NON-COMPETITIVE INTERESTS

This second postulate aims to correct the evils arising from the competition for economic goods. Professor Hocking states it as follows: *"Every competitive interest must be so transformed or interpreted as to be non-competitive, or an ingredient in a non-competitive interest."* (*Idem*, p. 227) But further on he admits that many competitive interests can never be completely transformed, but can only become ingredients in a non-competitive interest. And this admission is extremely important when we try to set up a mechanism through which the requirements of this postulate can be met. For we need only to show that competitive interests can be so interpreted as to become ingredients in a non-competitive interest. This is possible whereas the complete transformation into a non-competitive interest would not be in every case. However, it would be possible in some cases, and hence the postulate must be worded to cover both possibilities.

A typical example of a competitive value would

be money, since it is the medium for the exchange of all kinds of economic goods. The interest men have in accumulating money is a competitive interest. On the other hand, original ideas are non-competitive values, and one's interest in promulgating such ideas is a non-competitive interest. In general, all consumable goods are competitive values whereas all cultural values are non-competitive. In using the former I exclude others from using those same goods that I use or consume, but when I participate in the enjoyment of cultural values I do not exclude others from participating. And when I create a new idea which adds even a tiny bit to human cultural value, my own power is enhanced by sharing this idea with others. For all of those who use my idea thereby augment my influence at the same time that they increase their own. Hence it is obvious that the evils arising from the competition for economic goods would be checked, if people would subordinate the pursuit of such goods to the pursuit of cultural values. If we could bring about such a transformation of competitive into non-competitive interests in large numbers of individuals, then we would have an ideal state from the standpoint of the second evil.

To illustrate this process let us imagine a person starting out in life with a deep sense of need for money. Assume that he has awakened to a realization of the fact that in a capitalistic society money is an indispensable medium for securing the various goods which he needs for himself and family. Such

POSTULATES OF AN IDEAL STATE

a person will normally begin the mad rush to accumulate property in some form or another so as to make himself and his family reasonably secure. This pursuit of wealth to satisfy bodily and other needs may be continued throughout life without the person ever becoming aware that there are more intrinsic values that a man may seek. But when it is successful in a large way, and the man who is now rich begins to reflect upon his continual pursuit of money beyond what is necessary to supply the needs of himself and his family, the meaning of wealth may change. The rich man soon discovers that money gives power over others, and then he may begin the quest for the power that great wealth gives to its owner. But the pursuit of wealth to secure one against the slings and arrows of outrageous fortune, and the pursuit of wealth for power are entirely different forms of the interest in competitive value. Nevertheless, both of these forms are highly competitive. But suppose now that a reflecting rich man is led to the further transformation of his interest in money to that of using it to promulgate ideas and for the welfare of others. Then he will make the surprising discovery that the power of ideas is greater than the power of wealth, and is *ultimately the only justification for the continual, life-long pursuit of wealth*. By this process the purely competitive interest in wealth can be completely transformed into the non-competitive love of ideas.

Why should the possibility of such a transformation be restricted to those few reflective rich men who become philanthropists and patrons of science and the arts? What mechanism in a social order would make this transformation possible for large numbers of individuals? Obviously cultural values must be conserved and continually enhanced, since the interest in economic values has to be transformed in some way into an interest in them. But "art is long and time is fleeting." The individual life-span is relatively short. Culture would be pitifully small in amount and insignificant in value if it had to be born anew and die with each generation. In order that culture may exist and transcend the separate life-spans of individuals, there must be cultural continuity from one generation to another through many generations. What would Einstein's science be without that of Galileo and Newton? Yet both of these men were dead when Einstein was born. What would modern music be without classical music? Every aspect of culture —science, religion, art—is of much longer duration than the life-span of even the oldest individuals. So our second postulate can be met only in those social orders in which cultural values are conserved. This is another proof that man needs the state, since without it there is no guarantee that cultural values will be conserved.

It follows that an ideal state would be one which stressed cultural rather than economic values. It would be one in which economic values were duly subordinated to cultural values, one in which indi-

POSTULATES OF AN IDEAL STATE

viduals were more interested in contributing to and in conserving culture than they were in making money, and in accumulating wealth. It would be one in which all competitive interests could really become ingredients in some non-competitive interest, and not one in which who gets what, and when, and how, are the dominant interests. Yet Professor Hocking is undoubtedly right in adding this qualifying paragraph: "Such transformation, however, would be gradual in an ideal state,—still more so in any actual state, where the results of competition are still governed by many factors irrelevant to personal worth. Where the game retains the general character of 'grab,' competition will keep its predominantly exclusive quality and its primitive meaning: my gain is your loss. Hence the deformity of human nature in the state is not a myth: we can only say that it would be still more deformed apart from it, and only by its aid can it become less deformed."[3] Statesmen must find ways to correct these evils. They must provide for such a system of distributing wealth as will best minister to the conservation and enhancement of culture. They must assure to all the opportunity to participate in the enjoyment of cultural values. And most important of all, they must create an effective way of selecting from among young people those most capable of doing creative work in the various fields of culture.

[3] *Loco citato*, p. 237.

4. THE POSTULATE OF CONSTRUCTIVE CRITICISM

We need a postulate to correct the evils that arise from the fixity and rigidity of institutions. Professor Hocking states his third postulate as follows: *"Whatever in institutions tends at any time to deform human nature shall be freely subject to the force of dissatisfaction naturally directed to change them."* I call this principle the postulate of constructive criticism since it obviously assumes that the critic is a person of good will, who is really primarily interested in correcting their defects rather than in completely destroying institutions. Undoubtedly some institutions within a state and occasionally even some states outlive their usefulness. They become so static and fixed that they are actually moribund. Against such institutions an individual has a right to rebel. However, most institutions are merely defective and the postulate assumes that their defects can be corrected by affected individuals bringing the force of their criticism to bear upon them.

According to Plato's *Apology*, Socrates considered himself to be the gadfly of ancient Athens. His function was to sting the sluggish state into action by the shafts of his criticisms. And every institution and the state itself needs some effective gadfly to sting it into efficacious activity. In the modern world this postulate can be met by granting freedom of speech to all who have complaints. A free press, a free radio, a free public forum where every Tom, Dick and Harry can make his own soap box oration, and tell what he thinks is wrong with social institutions, is the mechanism essential to the proper functioning of this postulate. Without free and outspoken criticisms, through the various media of public communication, there is no way in which the force of criticism can be directed towards the evils in institutions. So a state that leaves its citizens as free as possible in the expression of their criticisms is the ideal state from the point of view of the third evil. And yet the evils due to the fixity of institutions will never be corrected by criticism alone, since unanswered criticism would soon undermine the institutions and destroy them. But in healthy institutions criticisms never long remain unanswered.

5. The Postulate of Conserving Force

Critics of institutions should always remember that others participate in the activities of that institution besides themselves, and they must expect their criticisms to be met by those who value the institution. Those who are conscious of receiving benefits from an institution have a right to fight for its preservation. They will endeavor to strengthen it against its critics. Many of them will go too far, as in the famous toast: "Here is to my country, may she ever be right, but my country—right or wrong!" If an ideal state is one which fosters criticism, it must also provide for the conservation of the known values of the institutions which are continually being subjected to criticism.

Thus we require a fourth postulate to counteract the third. Professor Hocking states it like this: *"Conserving force shall be proportionate to certainty."* I call this the postulate of conserving force. It means that everyone benefiting from an institution shall be given the right to defend that institution to the extent that he is certain of its value. Reformers and radicals have a right to criticize, but conservatives have a right to defend. And they should be given as free use of all the various forms of communication as is given the critics.

Thus the third and fourth postulates can both be realized through the same mechanism. One operates as a check on the other. If all criticism of institutions, be they political, economic, or cultural, is shut off, the evils resulting from the internal corruption of these institutions will multiply like maggots. If all propaganda in defense of institutions is forbidden, then these institutions will be devoured by their critics as a field of grain is devoured by a hungry swarm of grasshoppers. A proper balance must be maintained between the critics of institutions and the propagandists for institutions, if the evils in them are to be continually checked and corrected.

An ideal state will be one which is so organized as to maintain a balance between critics and conservators. Such a state will have a machinery for dealing with the third type of evil. Its citizens will remain virile, conscious of their liberties, zealous for their rights. Such a people cannot be enslaved

POSTULATES OF AN IDEAL STATE 59

by any other people. Their strength will be so great that no other state will dare to attack them.

We have now described an ideal state as one embodying the four postulates and we have indicated the mechanisms essential to the normal functioning of these postulates. Such a state would be ideal in the sense that it would offer a perpetual check on the three evils. But note that this conception of an ideal state is genuinely realistic in that it recognizes that none of these three kinds of evils can be entirely eliminated, since they are inherent in the very nature of community life.

6. FIVE JURAL POSTULATES

In stating and interpreting Professor Hocking's four postulates we have defined a set of ethical principles to meet the three kinds of evils inherent in any social order. A state embodying these principles could certainly be regarded as an ideal state with respect to such evils. But there are other points of view from which a definition of an ideal state can be approached, and an especially interesting and significant one is the legal point of view.

In his *Law and Rights* Professor Hocking lays down the basic ethical principle of the philosophy of law which is "the natural right of the individual to become what he is capable of becoming." From this very general norm he derives two sets of essential rights. One of these sets is *the right to liberty*. It consists of three special rights: (1) the liberty of each individual to manage himself, (2) to seek whatever control over others he is capable of exercising for their good, and (3) to control the forces and resources of nature so far as is within his power. The second set is *the right to security*. Everyone has (1) the right to the security of his person, (2) of his agreements and contracts, and (3) of his private property. These two sets of three each are permanent rights which belong to every civilized person, and every such person should be able to claim such rights from his own state. Hence it follows that an ideal state will be one that is so constituted legally as to guarantee these essential human rights.

Dean Roscoe Pound has stated a set of five jural postulates which would guarantee these rights. He originally formulated them with special reference to American society, but they can be generalized and treated as the basic ethical assumptions on which all law rests.

Jural Postulate I

"In civilized society men must be able to assume that others will commit no intentional aggressions upon them."

Jural Postulate II

"In civilized society men must be able to assume that they may control for beneficial purposes what they have discovered and appropriated to their own use, what they have created by their own labor, and what they have acquired under the existing social and economic order."

POSTULATES OF AN IDEAL STATE

Jural Postulate III

"In civilized society men must be able to assume that those with whom they deal in the general intercourse of society will act in good faith, and hence,

(a) will make good reasonable expectations which their promises or other conduct reasonably create;

(b) will carry out their undertakings according to the expectations which the moral sentiment of the community attaches thereto;

(c) will restore specifically or by equivalent what comes to them by mistake or unanticipated situation, whereby they receive what they could not reasonably have expected to receive under the actual circumstances."

Jural Postulate IV

"In civilized society men must be able to assume that others, when they act affirmatively, will do so with due care with respect to consequences that may reasonably be anticipated."

Jural Postulate V

"In civilized society men must be able to assume that others who maintain things likely to get out of hand or to escape and do damage will restrain them or keep them within their proper bounds." [4]

These five jural postulates can also be used to define an ideal state. Such a state would be one

[4] Quoted by W. E. Hocking in *Law and Rights*, pp. 93 f. (Yale University Press), from Dean Roscoe Pound's *Introduction to American Law* (Dunster House Bookshop, Cambridge, Mass., 1919).

having a detailed system of law and an elaborate set of institutions based upon these jural postulates. It would seem that any civilized society should recognize some such ethical principles as the underlying basis of all law and order.

The next chapter contains an analysis of the structure of the ideal state. After this analysis is made we propose to use the four postulates of the ideal state as criteria to evaluate certain actual states (Chapters V-VII). It would complicate our discussion unduly should we also use the jural postulates for this purpose. Moreover this is hardly necessary, since the jural postulates are implicit in the structure of the ideal state, and we plan to use the elements of that structure as criteria along with the four postulates. This will be clear to the reader if he will take the various institutions, making up the three orders distinguished in the next chapter, to be the concrete forms which the jural postulates take in a civilized community. We plan, then, to use the three orders of the ideal state as criteria in evaluating actual states instead of the five jural postulates.

What to Read

On *Utopia* see the article with this title in the 14th edition of the *Encyclopedia Britannica* and the references there given. See also J. O. Hertzler: *History of Utopian Thought*. There are selections from Francis Bacon's *New Atlantis* and T. Campanella's *City of the Sun* in D. S. Robinson's *An Anthology of Modern Philosophy*, pp. 62-86.

POSTULATES OF AN IDEAL STATE

The article entitled *Communism* in Hastings' *Encyclopedia of Religion and Ethics* is also valuable.

See Immanuel Kant's *Critique of the Practical Reason,* Bk. II, Ch. II, Sections IV-VI, for his postulates of morality, translated by T. K. Abbott in *Kant's Moral Philosophy.* See D. S. Robinson: *An Anthology of Modern Philosophy,* pp. 494 ff., and W. M. Urban: *Fundamentals of Ethics,* Ch. XV.

In addition to the references to W. E. Hocking and Dean Pound already given, on ideals see the article entitled *Ideals* in Hastings' *Encyclopedia of Religion and Ethics,* Vol. VII, pp. 86 ff.; M. C. Otto: *Things and Ideals;* John Dewey: *Human Nature and Conduct,* Chs. VI and VII; T. H. Green: *Prolegomena to Ethics,* Bk. III.

On freedom of opinion and speech see F. W. Coker: *Recent Political Thought,* pp. 385-407 (with a select bibliography). John Stuart Mills' essay on *Liberty* is a classic in this field. See also Zechariah Chafee, Jr.: *Freedom of Speech;* Herbert Hoover: *The Challenge to Liberty;* Horace M. Kallen: *Freedom in the Modern World;* H. J. Laski: *Liberty in the Modern State;* Walter Lippmann: *The Method of Freedom;* Everett Dean Martin: *Liberty;* John A. Ryan: *Declining Liberty and Other Papers.* See the references at the end of the next chapter.

CHAPTER IV

THE THREE ORDERS OF AN IDEAL STATE

1. THE PRIVATE ORDER

In the first part of the preceding chapter an ideal state was defined which would constitute a permanent check on the three kinds of evils inherent in any social order. Four postulates were stated and the mechanism for the realization of each was explained, and it was argued that a state in which these postulates were effectively functioning would be an actualization of such an ideal state.

In this chapter we propose to define the ideal state that can be actualized by analyzing the social structure from the standpoint of what is needed to give human beings adequate opportunity for the fullest possible development of their own nature. What structure must the social order as a whole have, if it is to satisfy the deepest aspirations and the most insistent needs of normal human beings? Here we are raising this question with special reference to human beings of a highly civilized type. We are not thinking of savages and extremely backward peoples. What organization of the total social environment is required for the well-rounded and fullest possible development of the citizen par-

THREE ORDERS OF AN IDEAL STATE 65

ticipating in that environment? The answer to this question will give us an analysis of the ideal state from the point of view of its structure. The ideal state defined by this analytical method of approach will not be essentially different from the one constituted by the four postulates and their respective mechanisms. The analytical approach will stress the values men seek and find in and through the various institutions of organized society, whereas the other approach especially emphasized the correction of the three kinds of evils inherent in social organizations. The two approaches give us different aspects of the same ideal state rather than two entirely opposite conceptions of what such a state would be.

Generally speaking, all normal human beings have in them a deep desire to be appreciated for what they are. They long to be loved and to have intimate relations with others whom they can love. Love is more, far more, than the so-called gregarious or herd instinct among animals. Nor can it be identified with the bonds of tribal emotion which hold savage groups together. The gregarious instinct and the kinship ties among savages are at best but faint anticipations of the principle of love as it operates among highly civilized people. Love includes sex-love but it has other forms. Driven by this urge men demand a set of social institutions through which it can find complete expression and realization. Let us call this set of institutions that is founded upon human love the *private order*.

The *family* is the basic institution of the private order, and the experience of the race proclaims the permanent monogamous family as the highest form of the family. In spite of numerous exceptions it continues to be true of the majority in complex industrial societies that membership in a permanent monogamous family offers, both to men and to women, the best scope for the expression and satisfaction of sex-love, and its sub-forms—parental and filial love.

Nevertheless, it would be a serious error to identify the private order with the family. For there are various other institutions through which human beings are able to satisfy the craving for appreciation from others. Polite society and fraternities of all kinds must be included as important institutions constituting the private order. Men and women form these institutions to give full scope for the exercise of that deep craving in them for intimate association with a few of their fellows to whom they can give and from whom they can claim sympathy, appreciation, and love. Here, too, should be placed the various recreational and amusement associations. Golf clubs, athletic associations, riding academies, bridge clubs, racing associations—what are these and their likes but other ways in which men and women may find a scope for the full realization of a side of their nature which craves an outlet and an adequate arena for its complete satisfaction?

Now an ideal society must be one in which such

THREE ORDERS OF AN IDEAL STATE

institutions are fostered and are made and kept as strong and as wholesome as possible. The state which seeks to destroy those human institutions making up the private order is working against itself. For every person gains the strength and also the incentive for living from his participation in the private order. Normally its institutions renew the energies of men and add meaning and zest to life. Thus the ideal state will be one which protects and supports by constructive measures the institutions constituting the private order.

2. The Public Order

On the other hand, every normal human being is driven by an urge which for want of a better name we may call *ambition*. Shakespeare has Wolsey say to Cromwell:

> Fling away ambition;
> By that sin fell the angels.

And he puts into the mouth of Macbeth the well known lines:

> I have no spur
> To prick the sides of my intent, but only
> Vaulting ambition, which o'erleaps itself
> And falls on the other side.

Many share this idea that ambition is a sin that will destroy him who is dominated by it.

This conception of ambition stresses that type of person who allows his ambition to dominate every other side of his nature. Ambition is good when it is held in check. Without it men sink to a low level of mediocrity. Such ambitionless human beings are either moronic and abnormal or lazy and shiftless. The average human being feels within himself an urge to spend his energies in some kind of effective work in the world. Such men find in the world of affairs, of politics and of business, an arena for the realization of this side of their nature. Let us call the various institutions through which ambition is realized the *public order*.

The nation in action, *the actual state,* constitutes the fundamental institution of the public order. In its own functioning it provides the means whereby numerous individuals may realize their highest ambition. Public office remains for many youths the supreme goal of life. Inspired by great statesmen and judges there are large numbers of young people today who are preparing themselves so that they may fill these positions creditably. In perpetuating itself the state provides all kinds of avenues for advancement, and for the realization of special ambitions of countless thousands. Think of the civil service field of employment, of the opportunities offered to youth by the Army and the Navy, by various educational and research institutions supported by national, state, and local governments, and you will realize how important every actual state is in providing for thousands of its citizens a real field in which they may realize their ambitions.

Yet the state is by no means the only institution

forming the public order, or, at any rate, it need not be. There are innumerable privately owned institutions which are essential parts of the public order in some actual states. Theoretically there is no reason why one should treat the totalitarian conception of the state as the only adequate conception. Which type of actual state is best will be considered later. Here we must stick to the facts and insist that the public order may and often does include other institutions than the state. And when it does all of these institutions provide further opportunities for the realization of ambition. Think, for example, of the many big and little business corporations, of the large number of trades, and of the trade unions which develop with the several trades, and of the various trade associations. All these form parts of the public order. It is convenient to group together, under the general name *politico-economic institutions,* all of the institutions making up the public order.

The truly ideal state must be one in which the politico-economic institutions are so deeply entrenched as to form in their entirety an adequate arena in which the average citizen may realize his ambition. That is an unjust social order in which large numbers of men and women find it impossible to secure employment. The state must be so well organized that it can give its citizens all kinds of opportunities for the realization of their ambitions. Unless it is so organized crime will breed rapidly and gangsters, bandits, and racketeers will destroy the state. We cannot question the right of people to labor. Ambition demands and will find an outlet. It has created innumerable institutions in the course of human history for its own realization, and it has destroyed institutions which have prevented its expression. What human ambition has done it can do again, and it will. Men must have an adequate scope for the full realization of ambition.

3. Relations of the Public and Private Orders to Each Other

After expounding the two orders somewhat as has just been done, Professor Hocking says: "The direct question: Which is your more real self, that of the public or that of the private order? most persons would find it hard to answer. It may be that the sexes differ in their natural finding of the dominating order. But for both men and women, both orders are necessary to a complete personality, and in the arrangements of life, each order, and each passion, takes its turn at hegemony. The honors are divided by alternation, and not by a disjunctive choice."[1] And then he proceeds to explain why the average human being's life has to alternate between the two orders.

The basic reason is that such an alternation is a psychological necessity. One order supplements the other. The person who restricts his activities to the private order develops the vices of the over-

[1] W. E. Hocking: *Human Nature and Its Remaking,* 2nd ed., p. 308, Yale University Press.

THREE ORDERS OF AN IDEAL STATE

domesticated and effeminate man. He becomes soft and flabby like a plant raised in a hothouse. On the other hand, exclusive devotion to the public order hardens men and makes them callous to all the finer sensibilities. Such men become mere cogs in a great machine. Their lives are reduced to a purely mechanical routine, and all the meaning they should find in their daily living seeps away. Healthy mindedness cannot exist unless one can in some way vary his activities so as to participate in both orders. This is what is meant by saying that it is a psychological necessity that men alternate between the two orders in such a way as to participate in the values of each.

In the public order a man markets whatever talents he happens to possess. He sells his service but retains his own point of view and unique outlook on life. But unless he has some one near to him who appreciates him for what he is, rather than for what he can do in the public order, he will develop a certain spirit of surrender, an inferiority complex, if you prefer that expression, which will make it impossible for him to succeed in the public order. Slowly his effectiveness will ebb away, and he will either be relegated to the insignificant positions in the public order, or he will join the crowd of misfits and ne'er-do-wells. It is only because of the qualities of character which he gets from participating in the private order that any person can succeed permanently in the public order.

On the other hand, unless a man has some anchorage in the public order where he can market his peculiar talents he will be a failure in the private order. The best friends and the best lovers are those who are independently real, who are conscious of their own power to achieve a place that is worth while in the public order. We learn from experience that people who are misfits in the public order have very little to give to their intimate friends and relatives. One has to achieve something in the arena of public life in order to be of any real value to the members of his own family and to his friends.

So we may lay down two basic propositions: (1) Success in the public order depends upon an individual's having a certain quality of mind and character which is developed primarily by participation in the private order. (2) Success in the private order depends upon an individual's winning for himself an honorable place in the public order. Hence it is necessary for each individual to live in such a way that some of his time and energy is devoted to the public order and some of it to the private order. A perpetual alternation between the two orders is required for the maintenance of a balanced life. And the ideal state must be one which recognizes this psychological necessity for the alternation of human activities, and accordingly provides for and supports both orders. No man can fully realize himself in one of these orders to the exclusion of the other.

Are these two orders sufficient to satisfy all the

needs of men? Many thinkers would answer yes. Granted that a proper balance is maintained between the two orders, they think that men can find complete satisfaction by dividing their activities between participating in the public order and participating in the private order. But such a view of human nature, and of what will satisfy human nature, is not profound enough. For there is more in men than can find adequate release in the public and private orders. A society in which the politico-economic institutions and those of the private order were perfectly developed would not really give to its members an adequate scope for the realization of that which is most unique in them. For the release of that residual uniqueness another order is required.

4. The Cultural Order

Let us assume that there is a *creative urge* in every normal human being, which drives him forward in the effort to weave into the fabric of the universe his own unique contribution.

> Ah Love! could you and I with Fate conspire,
> To grasp this sorry Scheme of Things entire,
> Would not we shatter it to bits—and then
> Remould it nearer to the Heart's Desire!

The Heart's Desire—what is it? It is more than love, for it would subordinate love to the task of remoulding the world. It is more than ambition for it would shatter the sorry Scheme of Things in which ambition seeks to realize itself, and remould it. There is in every man a deeper longing, a profounder yearning than love or ambition. This eagerness to make one's own unique contribution to the universe can never find complete satisfaction either in the institutions of the private or in those of the public order. For this creative urge is the basis of the *cultural order*.

In olden times the basic institution of the cultural order was *organized religion*. Religion then fostered the various aspects of culture, and it still promises to men the widest scope for the realization of that residual part of their nature which remains unsatisfied in the private and public orders. However, religion has produced an offspring of cultural functions which today threaten her hegemony. Art offers to men a world of the imagination in which they have an unlimited scope for creativity. Science opens up a field of exploration which gives release to many of the hidden powers of men. Now each of these activities has created a large number of institutions in which cultural values are conserved and enhanced. Art museums and art colonies, religious retreats, sacred assemblies and councils, scientific laboratories and natural history museums, associations of various learned professions, institutes, academies—these and other institutions are all vital parts of the social order as a whole, and yet in their totality they form an order that is beyond society defined in terms of the public and private orders.

THREE ORDERS OF AN IDEAL STATE 75

Why do men need the cultural order for complete self-realization? Because their creative urge drives them on and on, and there must be some realm in which this urge can find its complete realization. No restrictions should be placed on the human urge to creativity. Cultural institutions must be maintained, no matter what the cost, to provide opportunities for gifted individuals to give complete and adequate expression to their specific talents. Nor should cultural values be available only to the few who are gifted. Those who cannot create such values must be permitted to share in them, thereby enriching their lives with new vistas and escaping from the humdrum of bodily existence. Without a vision of the higher values conserved by the cultural order the masses would sink back into barbarism. The ideal state will be one in which the cultural order is given its rightful place of superiority over the other two orders.

5. Relation of the Cultural to the Other Two Orders

Modern life is highly secularized. As was stated above the public order and the private order are thought by many to be completely independent and self-sufficient. Such thinkers see no valid reason for setting the cultural order apart as essentially independent of the other two. They would merge art and science with the public order, and substitute an urbane humanism and a benevolent philanthropy for religion. To them the cultural order lacks the essential material basis of the public and private orders, and is too intangible to be real except as an aspect or phase of one or the other or both of these orders. Does this notion that the cultural order can be dispensed with as a separate order give due recognition to its importance and its place in human experience as a whole?

Let us look at the matter genetically and historically. Among the earlier civilized peoples we find one order dominant. Such social orders are usually theocratic. The private order is wholly under the domination of religion. So also is the public order. Priests rule. A contemporary example of such a theocratic state is the backward nation, Thibet, ruled by a Grand Lama of the corrupt Buddhistic cult known as Lamaism, which is the religion of that benighted land. Among more enlightened peoples the public and private orders have emancipated themselves from priestly domination. Nevertheless history shows that originally there was only one order and that the private and public orders arose out of this matrix. And this can only mean that they were formerly dependent on the cultural order. From the historical point of view there can be no question about that, even though it must be freely admitted that civilization has been made possible and enriched by their emancipation.

Logically, the public and the private orders are today even more dependent on the cultural order

THREE ORDERS OF AN IDEAL STATE

than their defenders like to admit. For we learned that those two orders are incapable of standing on their own feet and that each uses qualities of men that are produced in the other order. Now we are in a position to see that the ultimate source of these qualities is the cultural order. Men succeed in the private and in the public order because they can participate in the cultural order. A generation which concludes that the world has lied to its saints and sages is a generation that has lost its knowledge of the source of values and its standard for ranking values. There are two basic principles or norms contributed by the cultural order to abandon which would mean to turn downward from the apex of civilization. These principles are: (i) *The sources of value must be put above specific values*, and (ii) *Personality must be put above property*. Adherence to these principles produces in men the kind of character which will enable them to take their places in the private and public orders. A state that turns its back on these basic principles derived from the cultural order is already decaying, because it lacks the leadership essential to its own continuance.

So we must conclude that the ideal state will be one in which the cultural order is given the primacy over the other two orders, no matter how necessary both of them may be. To turn away from it is to turn toward an ultimate relapse into barbarism.

Diagram of the Three Orders

Cultural Order

Based on urge to creativity

Fundamental institutions – those of religion, art, and science

Private Order

Based on love

Fundamental institutions –
Family
Fraternities
Service Clubs
Recreational Groups

Public Order

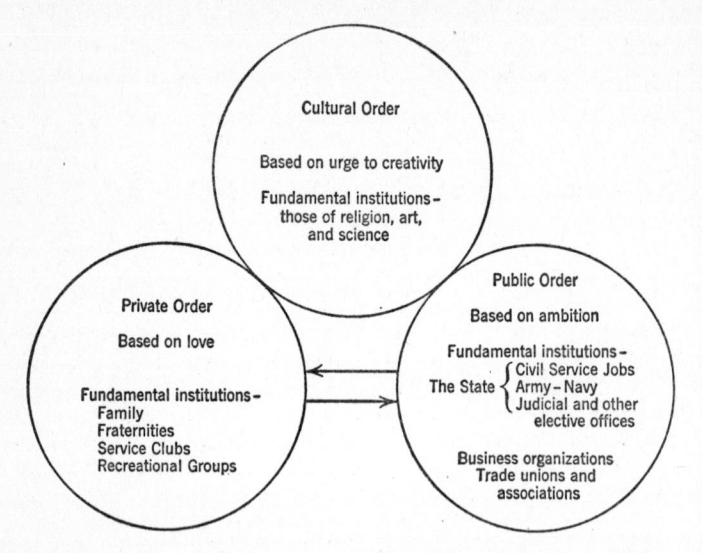

Based on ambition

Fundamental institutions –
The State { Civil Service Jobs
Army – Navy
Judicial and other elective offices

Business organizations
Trade unions and associations

A Diagram of the Three Orders.

In the diagram the cultural order is put at the top to indicate its primacy over the other two orders, and each of them is represented as touching it to show that they originated from it. The arrows indicate that the public and private orders are reciprocally dependent. The ideal social order is one consisting of all three orders, with the public and private orders duly subordinated to the cultural order.

Summarizing what has been said in these two chapters on the ideal state, we have expounded three definite and precise sets of principles, conformity to which would make any social order ethical from the standpoint of its relation to its own members. To the extent that any actual state conforms to the four postulates, and embodies the mechanisms essential to their proper functioning, such a state will be ethical because it will offer a constant check on the three

THREE ORDERS OF AN IDEAL STATE

kinds of evils inherent in any organized human society. To the extent that any actual state incorporates in its structure the five jural postulates of Dean Pound it will be ethical because it will guarantee to its citizens the essential rights of liberty and security. And to the extent that any actual state maintains a proper balance and harmony of the three orders, it will be ethical because it will provide for every one of its nationals an equal opportunity to appreciate and to enjoy a rich variety of values, as well as to contribute his bit to the creative process whereby these values are permanently enriched and conserved.

WHAT TO READ

For the distinction between civilization and culture and a discussion of various theories of culture see below, Chapter IX. On the three orders see the articles entitled *Family, State,* and *Culture,* in Hastings' *Encyclopedia of Religion and Ethics* (Vol. V, pp. 716 ff.; Vol. XI, pp. 814 ff.; Vol. IV, pp. 358 ff.). On culture see the article entitled *Anthropology* in the 14th edition of the *Encyclopedia Britannica.* R. C. Cabot's *What Men Live By* is an excellent popular account. W. M. Urban's *Fundamentals of Ethics,* Chaps. XII-XIII, gives a good exposition of the economic order and of the family.

The following books are also valuable: Adolf A. Berle and Gardiner C. Means: *The Modern Corporation and Private Property;* C. Deslie Burns: *Industry and Civilization;* S. Parkes Cadman: *Christianity and the State,* Lecture III; Stuart Chase: *The Economy of Abundance;* John M. Clark: *Social Control of Business;* John Dewey and J. H. Tufts:

Ethics (Revised ed.); Wallace B. Donham: *Business Looks at the Unforeseen;* W. Y. Elliott: *The Pragmatic Revolt in Politics,* Ch. XII; Felix Frankfurter: *The Public and Its Government;* L. T. Hobhouse: *The Elements of Social Justice;* W. E. Hocking: *Man and the State,* Pt. II; Jacob H. Hollander: *Economic Liberalism;* John M. Keynes: *The End of Laissez-faire;* J. Kohler: *Philosophy of Law* (English translation); Walter Lippmann: *The Method of Freedom,* Ch. II; R. M. MacIver: *The Modern State,* Ch. I; F. Paulsen: *Ethics,* Bk. III, Ch. V. (English translation); Sir Arthur Salter: *The Framework of an Ordered Society;* Sumner H. Slichter: *Modern Economic Society;* G. M. Stratton: *Experimental Psychology and Its Bearing upon Culture;* George Soule: *A Planned Society;* R. H. Tawney: *The Acquisitive Society;* James H. Tufts: *The Real Business of Living,* Pt. II; Henry A. Wallace: *New Frontiers;* Graham Wallas: *Our Social Heritage;* Woodrow Wilson: *The New Freedom.*

CHAPTER V

CONFORMITY OF ACTUAL STATES TO THE IDEAL: THE SOVIET STATE

1. THE PROBLEM STATE

We now have to attempt what many may regard as the audacious undertaking of evaluating actual states by applying to them the two sets of criteria which have been worked out in setting up the ideal state. We shall first inquire whether, or to what extent, typical actual states embody the four postulates and the mechanism for their proper functioning. And then we shall inquire whether, or to what extent, typical actual states recognize the three orders of an ideal social order, and the institutions which each of these orders creates in the effort to satisfy the deeper needs of men; and whether actual states strive to maintain a proper balance between these three orders.

No doubt such an attempt really is audacious in the sense that it can only be provisional. Then, too, there is bound to be some arbitrariness in the evaluations that are made. And yet the application of these two definite sets of criteria to actual states does promise to bring some clarity into a hopelessly confused situation. Even though there may be other ways of evaluating actual states than those determined by these two sets of criteria, and even though some thinkers may prefer some of these other ways, nevertheless here are two very definite and precise sets of criteria which can be used for this purpose, and they do give us a clue to the ethical value of actual existing states. Admitting, then, the audaciousness of the undertaking, we will attempt it because it at least promises to clarify the issues. Moreover, it offers a quite unique and precise method of reaching a fair and unbiased attitude toward actual states.

Spinoza, referring to governments as *Dominions,* classifies them into three distinct types. He writes: "Speaking generally, he holds dominion, to whom are entrusted by common consent affairs of state—such as the laying down, interpretation, and abrogation of laws, the fortification of cities, deciding on war and peace, etc. But if this charge belong to a council, composed of the general multitude, then the dominion is called a democracy; if the council be composed of certain chosen persons, then it is an aristocracy; and if, lastly, the care of affairs of state and, consequently, the dominion rest with one man, then it has the name of monarchy." [1] *Democracy, aristocracy,* and *monarchy* are the three types of state here recognized by Spinoza, but his classification is too simple for our day. A contemporary writer, Professor Robert M. MacIver, has

[1] Spinoza: *Political Treatise,* Ch. II, paragraph 17. (Elwes)

worked out a much more detailed classification of the various types of states, covering both the historical and contemporary forms, and it is reprinted below.

Professor MacIver's detailed classification is useful in showing all the various forms of actual states that have ever developed among the different major peoples of the earth. For our purpose it will be better to restrict the discussion to three distinct types, illustrating each with actual contemporary states. These are the conciliar dynastic or oligarchic type of state, represented among actual states

FORMS OF THE STATE

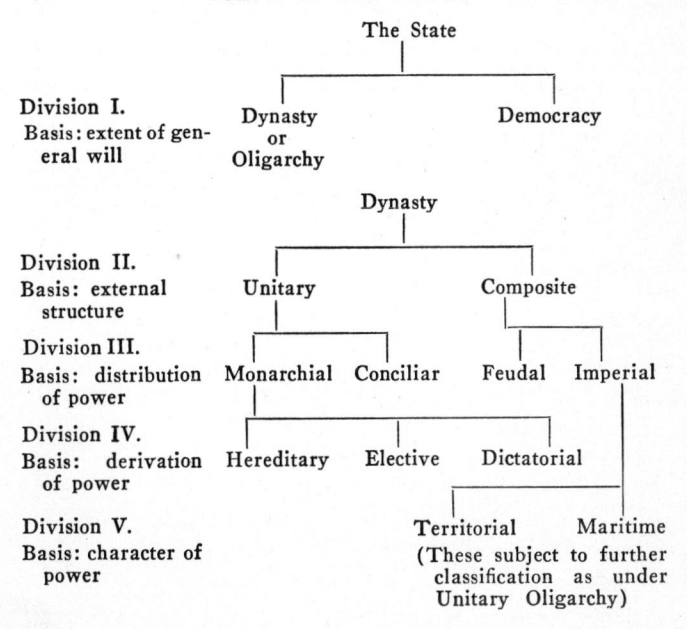

The State

Division I.
Basis: extent of general will

Dynasty or Oligarchy — Democracy

Dynasty

Division II.
Basis: external structure

Unitary — Composite

Division III.
Basis: distribution of power

Monarchial   Conciliar   Feudal   Imperial

Division IV.
Basis: derivation of power

Hereditary   Elective   Dictatorial

Division V.
Basis: character of power

Territorial   Maritime
(These subject to further classification as under Unitary Oligarchy)

FORMS OF THE STATE (continued)

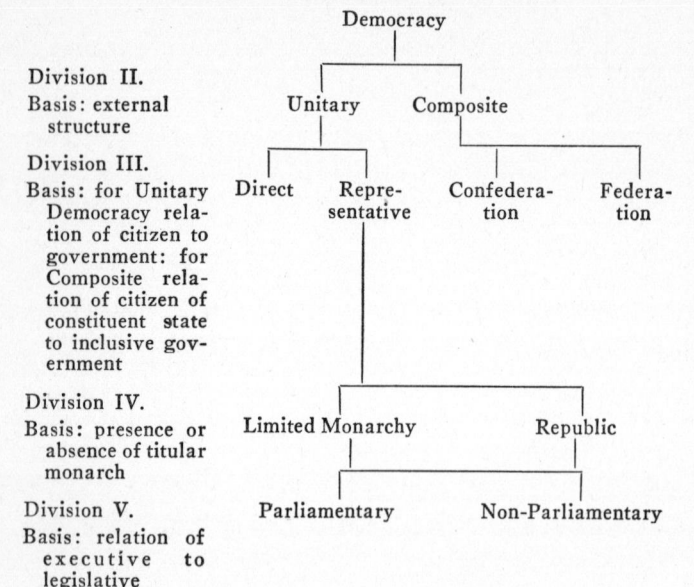

	Democracy	
Division II. Basis: external structure	Unitary / Composite	
Division III. Basis: for Unitary Democracy relation of citizen to government: for Composite relation of citizen of constituent state to inclusive government	Direct / Representative	Confederation / Federation
Division IV. Basis: presence or absence of titular monarch	Limited Monarchy	Republic
Division V. Basis: relation of executive to legislative	Parliamentary	Non-Parliamentary

In respect of composite states the term Democracy refers to the relation of the constituent states, not of the citizens, to the inclusive union. If that relation is a free one it is classified as Democracy, whatever the internal character of the constituents.—From Robert M. MacIver, *The Modern State*, p. 363. Reprinted by permission of the Oxford University Press.

by the Union of Socialist Soviet Republics; the monarchial oligarchy, represented by Fascism, and with which Nazism and other dictatorships may be included; and the representative type of democracy, exemplified in a somewhat different way by England, France, and the United States. In this chapter we shall be dealing with the Soviet State. A separate chapter will be devoted to Fascism and Nazism, and another to Representative Democracies.

2. Difficulty of Judging the Soviet State

Although some thinkers consider the Soviet State to be a special type of democracy, Professor MacIver classifies it as a conciliar oligarchy, which he says is a rare form of oligarchy. He justifies this opinion of the Soviet State in these words: "Conciliar oligarchy may also be classified on the same basis as unitary; in other words, the council may be hereditary or elective or it may constitute a dictatorship. We should characterize the soviet government of Russia as of the last-mentioned type. Nominally it is a 'dictatorship of the proletariat,' which means in effect the dictatorship of a small group based on proletarian support. It is a unique form, being a class-limited oligarchy which, unlike all other oligarchies, limits citizenship not from above, in the socio-economic sense, but from below. It is a form that could arise only in an oligarchical state, when a strongly oligarchical structure is so completely and suddenly overthrown that certain hitherto subject elements become dominant and apply the methods of their former masters."[2] This comment clearly indicates that the Soviet State is a unique type which has never existed before. And that is one reason why it is exceedingly difficult to apply the two sets of criteria to it.

Then, too, it is based upon the principle of violence. Originally the founders of the Soviet State had the idea that all other existing states must be overthrown in order for their type of state to come

[2] *Loco citato*, p. 348.

into existence. Later they came to recognize that they could create such a state within Russia without trying to overturn all other states. But Lenin's original idea is still operative, and his followers hope eventually to overcome all states by violence, then to create an ideal socialistic society by means of the Soviet State, after which they think that the Soviet State itself will disappear. Lenin wrote: "It is inconceivable that the Soviet Republic should continue to exist interminably side by side with imperialistic states. Ultimately one or the other must conquer. Pending this development a number of terrible clashes between the Soviet Republic and the bourgeoise states must inevitably occur." After quoting this statement Mr. William H. Chamberlin comments: "The menace of such an attack, of a renewal in some form or other of the wars of intervention which marked the first years of the existence of the Soviet Republic, is never absent. Therefore, the final victory of socialism, which will usher in the golden communist era of humanity, when armies, police, and all means of compulsion will be abolished and the state itself, in Lenin's phrase, will wither away because there will be no more of the class economic antagonisms which the state expresses—this final victory, then, can only be an international victory, the world revolution which is the Messianic hope of Russian Communists." [3] Here we have the characteristic Marxian

[3] William H. Chamberlin: *Soviet Russia,* p. 61. (Little, Brown and Company)

philosophy that condemns all existing states as hopelessly bad, that even admits that the Soviet State itself will finally wither away, and argues that mankind will live on the earth without the need of a state. It is difficult to apply criteria to determine the degree of goodness of a state whose founders have such a theoretical conception of what a state is, for the conception damns all existing states and even the Soviet State itself, whereas our criteria are based on the assumption that the state is an indispensable human institution.

In the third place the Soviet State is admittedly in its infancy. It doth not yet appear what it shall be. Undoubtedly it has a good lease on life and will continue in existence for many moons. And it is devoutly to be hoped that its latter stages will be increasingly better than its beginning stages. But so far it has to be judged on the basis of what it now is and what it has been during the nearly two decades of its existence. So the application of the criteria may not do justice to the Soviet State as it may later evolve.

3. Opposing Interpretations of the Importance of the Soviet State

In view of these three difficulties it is not surprising that thinkers differ in their evaluations of the significance of the Soviet State. While none doubt its importance, some regard it as the highest evolution the political state has attained, while others regard it as a veritable menace to civilization. Let us review these theories before stating our own view.

One theory is that the Soviet State will eventually conquer all other states, and that sovietism will become the organizing principle for a new supernational world order in which all men will dwell together in a unified communal life of a one hundred per cent pure socialistic and communistic type. Advocates of this view are doing all they can in France, in England, and in the United States to foment dissatisfaction with democracy because they think that "the badness of present states is more desirable than their goodness," that "the feeling of class hostility must be kept alive," that "appeals to ideals of justice must be read as a sign of cowardice"; that "mutual accommodation must be feared as a way to mutual degeneration," that "every concession should be met with greater demands"; that "every advance should be spurned, every gift spit upon, in order that the weakening enemy may not lose the war-like temper." [4] Surely this should be the attitude toward all other states, if one accepts the dogma that the Soviet State possesses an intrinsic ethical superiority over every other form of state and that every other form is inherently evil. Fortunately there are not many such rabid fanatics outside of Russia. But this fanatical attitude on the part of some admirers of the Soviet State has aroused an equally fervid antagonism against it. Doubtless

[4] W. E. Hocking: *Man and the State*, p. 450, Yale University Press.

THE SOVIET STATE 89

every fanatical communist in the world today could be paired with some equally fanatical defender of the *status quo* type of social order. No wonder there is a clash of opinions about the importance of the Soviet State!

More moderate opinions are doubtless nearer to the truth and such opinions are winning out everywhere, even in Russia. One of these is that represented by the great majority of the leaders of the communist party in Russia. They have decided that it is possible to create within Russia a completely socialistic state, and that such a state can be so strengthened internally that in the course of time it will outstrip economically the other actual states of the world. Those holding this view believe in adopting a conciliating attitude towards other states, they seek trade alliances with them and try in every way possible to cultivate friendly relations with the capitalistic countries. Yet they steadily maintain their purpose and bend all their energies in the direction of consolidating the victories won within Russia. Impartial observers of conditions within Russia, who are competent to judge, believe that this purpose can be accomplished in the course of a relatively long period of time.

Others hold that the Soviet State will gradually be transformed in the direction of capitalism and private ownership of property. They argue that certain changes have already taken place in this direction, for example, the New Economic Policy which restored to certain retailers the right to conduct private business. And they support this concrete evidence with the purely speculative idea that when wealth increases in Russia the stringent regulations will be modified in the direction of allowing individuals to own more property.

One or the other of these moderate views is doubtless true and will be proved true as time elapses. It is certainly ridiculous to imagine that the condition of people living in Russia today is superior to the present-day condition of people living in the regions of the earth dominated by all other types of states. All the evidence points to the fact that even the proletarian citizens of Russia—those not disenfranchised and occupying the most favored positions in the country—are really worse off today economically than almost any other civilized people on earth, the possible exceptions being the Chinese coolies and the Hindu outcastes. "There is a constant shortage of certain kinds of manufactured goods and a more or less sporadic shortage of certain food products," says Chamberlin. Although this was written in 1929 it still remains true that the Russian people are suffering all kinds of deprivations in the hope that the success of the noble experiment they are making will bring them better conditions of living. And this is generally admitted by those who know most about conditions within Russia. In view of these facts it is simply absurd to suppose that the average person in Russia is as well-off as the average person in England, France, or the United States, and it is unfair to the Soviet

State to compare it with these more advanced and more highly industrialized free nations. What we need to do is to compare the Soviet State with the old monarchial Russia of prewar days, since such a comparison will be much more favorable and will allow us to indicate definite values in the Soviet State as determined by our two sets of criteria.

4. Application of the Four Postulates to the Soviet State

(a) *The Postulate of Identical Ideals.*—Does the Soviet State allow its citizens to form definite ideals and does it permit them to work for the realization of the goals they have set before themselves? And does it allow the sentiment of admiration to function unhindered in the moulding of these ideals? In answer to these two questions it must be conceded that the Russian people are more unified than almost any other people on earth in the effort to realize the goal set by the leaders of the communist party as set forth in the so-called Five Year Plan. All the energies of the nation are directed in this channel, and every loyal Bolshevik is aflame with zeal for this national ideal.

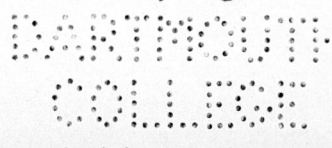

What is this national ideal? We must not make the mistake of thinking that it is wholly an economic policy, although that is certainly the part of the ideal that has been most stressed in western countries. The Bolshevik leaders recognize the importance of educating their young people in an absolutely new direction, so that they will "see everything from a new and entirely different point of view—not only things, but people as well." They are deliberately trying to make collectivists who hate people with property, internationalists who have a deep love for all working people everywhere, and militant atheists in whom "religious stupefaction" has been replaced by a knowledge of the laws of nature and of human society. This is the immediate threefold goal of the Five Year Plan on its educational side.

What is the ultimate goal which the Bolsheviks are setting before the youths of Russia whom they are training to be communists? It is the actualization of Lenin's purpose to create a classless society of workers, a new élite that shall destroy all other classes all over the world and ultimately dominate the whole earth. That Lenin's dream has not been entirely abandoned but has only been postponed until the dawning of a more opportune day is proven by the following passage, which is taken from a tract entitled: *The Communistic Education of Young Pioneers*. This tract was prepared by Mr. V. Hanchin for the instruction of leaders of the *Komsomols*, an organization of Russian youths similar to our Boy Scouts. Mr. Hanchin writes: "To train up a Communist means to develop a physically strong and healthy man. We need such men, for they will not be helpless in the fight with nature and in the armed struggle with the bourgeoisie. Our third generation will face this task. It will conduct the fight for the establishment of Communism in the whole world. This war will, of course, be with arms. We are not vegetarians; we know that the Old World can be reconstructed only with fire and sword. The third generation must be prepared for it.

"And so we need a Leninist who is aware of the course that the struggle will take, a warrior of the working class, a man with a strong will who is an irreconcilable fighter for the ideology of the proletariat, a collectivist, an internationalist, a militant atheist, a socially enterprising organizer, polytechnically trained and universally educated. Here is the new man; here is a Communist." [5] The phrase "polytechnically trained" refers to the Russian idea of training every worker so that he can perform many different functions in the state.

There is no doubt about the value of this ideal as a unifying principle, nor of its contribution to the success of the Soviet State. But its very success means that all other ideals are shoved into the background and completely subordinated to this one purpose. In other words, a purely socialistic economic ideal has replaced the numerous interested and disinterested ideals of our ideal social order, and all citizens are supposed to work towards its realization regardless of any other interests which they may have. It is an ideal which many have adopted as their own with fanatical enthusiasm, and yet it is an ideal imposed by the dictatorial powers of the authorities. In Russia education has

[5] *Character Education in Soviet Russia,* edited by William Clark Trow and translated by Paul D. Kalachov, pp. 35 f. (Ann Arbor Press, Ann Arbor, Michigan).

become almost entirely propaganda for this ideal. So the requirements of the postulate of identical ideals, achieved through the workings of the sentiment of admiration, can hardly be said to be met in the Soviet State.

(b) *The Postulate of the Transformation of Competitive into Non-Competitive Interests.*—The possibility of transforming competitive into non-competitive interests is not recognized by the leaders of the Soviet State. Their aim is to abolish all acquisition of property by individuals, and ultimately they hope to accomplish this purpose. For the present they recognize that the peasants cannot be dealt with in this way, so they permit some ownership of private property. In fact there are three types of organization among the peasants: the *commune*, the *artel*, and the *coöperative*. In the former there is practically complete socialization of private property. Members of a *commune* take their meals together and are allowed to keep only a few little articles for their own personal use. This form of organization would be the ideal, according to Marxian theory. The *artel* has proved more practicable and is now preferred by the leaders. The peasant is permitted to own his house and a small garden, and all small animals, but he must surrender his farm land, machinery, and working animals, and work with others under a director appointed by the state. But even this has been found to be too much to demand of all peasants. So the *coöperative* type of organization has been adopted in certain regions. Here peasants pool their land, machinery, and beasts of burden when they plant and harvest, without surrendering their title to this property as they must do in the artels. All three types are forms of collectivism, and most Russian peasants are collectivised in one or the other of these ways. It is estimated that 73.5% belong to artels, 18% to coöperatives, and only 8.5% to communes. There are also many large state-owned farms operated directly by the government with wage earners as laborers. These farms are financed by the government and the grain raised is exported. This shows that the Soviet State has not yet succeeded in rooting out of the peasants their acquisitive desires and competitive interests.

Moreover, collectivism has brought new difficulties with it. As yet the government has failed to establish a satisfactory balance between output of farm products and supply of needed manufactured goods for use of the peasants. In some districts the peasant is only allowed to spend about one-third of his income from his share of grain on such manufactured goods, and he is forced to do without many necessary articles. Then there are what are called "consuming tendencies" in collective farms, by which is meant all efforts of peasants to subordinate the interest of the state and of the collective group to their personal interests. For example, many peasants killed animals and ate them for meat when they were sorely needed for breeding and working purposes.

Thus the attempt of the Soviet State to eliminate competitive interests has not wholly succeeded, and has brought with it new problems. The new system does not adequately meet the demands of the second postulate. But in time it may succeed in overcoming the difficulties that have so far accompanied its application, and then citizens of Russia may be able to secure the necessary goods to maintain their lives and have much leisure time left for the pursuit of cultural values. Only time can tell whether the Soviet method is a better method of dealing with the evils inherent in competitive values than that of permitting the acquisition and ownership of private property. But so far it must be admitted that the Soviet State fails to meet the demands of the second postulate. In fact it has intensified the interest in competitive values by making an economic ideal basic in the life of the people.

(c) *The Postulates of Constructive Criticism and of Conserving Force.*—The postulate of constructive criticism is hardly allowed to function in the Soviet State at all. No criticism of the Soviet system is permitted. Freedom of speech and of the press does not exist in Russia. There is an elaborate espionage system, which functions so effectively that no citizen dares say anything against the methods or actions of the government. But the postulate of conserving force does work. There is an efficient system of propaganda which makes every citizen realize the importance of the Five Year Plan, and of making his own contribution to its realization. Thus the Soviet State fails to maintain a balance between the two postulates that correct the evils inherent in institutions. But again, it may later restore this balance as it becomes more stable and secure. So far it has been fighting for its very existence. Doubtless restrictions on freedom will gradually be relaxed. If so these two postulates will function more normally, and many of the evils in Soviet institutions will be corrected.

5. Application of the Three Orders to the Soviet State

Soviet leaders have made an attempt to subordinate the family as an institution to the state. One method used to do this has been to make divorce as easy as possible. In Russia either the husband or wife can secure a divorce by the simple process of filing with the authorities a statement that he or she no longer recognizes the marriage bonds, and in case there are children by arranging for their support. Another method of weakening the family has been the placing of women on an absolute equality with men in industry. Every married woman is supposed to be employed somewhere in addition to her home duties. And many of the functions of a private home have been transferred to public institutions. There are nurseries for the care of children and community kitchens for the preparation of food. Families are not often assembled in a single house. Many separate families are housed together, sometimes in one large room partitioned somewhat by the furniture. Thus there are numerous ways in which the family as an institution has been and is being weakened under the Soviet State.

This gradual weakening of the family will undoubtedly continue in Russia. Referring to the new cities which are to be one of the achievements of the Five Year Plan, Mr. Hanchin writes: "The new cities will bring about such drastic changes in life relationships that the words, 'my children' and 'my parents' will lose the meaning of ownership and will no longer be used. An entirely new scheme of life will develop when a family of several thousand people live in a commune, with all the children growing up together and every adult contributing his share for their education. For parents will rear and educate not only their own children but the children of the whole commune; they will see not only their own children, but a large group of them among whom theirs will be but a part; and all the children will participate in the work of the grown-ups, and by working among them will learn and gain experience." [6]

On the other hand, the other institutions of the private order have been strengthened. Recreational centers of all kinds have been created for working people. Palaces of the former rich merchants and nobles have been converted into living quarters and club rooms for working people. Hence the private order is recognized in the Soviet State. The leaders realize that people must alternate their activities

[6] *Loco citato*, pp. 28 f.

between work for the state and recreation. And the family as an institution has not been destroyed, nor is there any reason to believe that the authorities wish utterly to destroy it. They merely want to subordinate it to the state, and make it less private than it is in other actual states.

So far as the public order is concerned, our discussion of the application of the second postulate to the Soviet State indicates that the idea of the Bolsheviks is to absorb all economic organizations into the state. This even applies to the farms of the peasants. The authorities seek to control in detail all the wealth producing activities of the people. This is complete *socialism*. But their aim is also to regulate the distribution of this wealth so that everyone will receive his proportionate share as determined by his needs and the needs of the Five Year Plan for the state as a whole. This is *communism*. The goal of the Soviet State is the union of socialism and communism, and the making of the state both the producer and the distributor of all economic goods. Obviously this entirely upsets the balance between the political and the economic institutions making up the public order of the ideal state. In spite of Lenin's idea that the state must ultimately wither away in a classless society, in actual practice the Soviet State is omnipotent within Russia. Needless to say, this leads to bureaucracy, and to the many deadening defects inherent in any bureaucratic regime. The state weakens itself when it tries to destroy all the other institutions of the public order.

In like manner the cultural order is wholly subordinated to the economic and political ends of the Soviet State. All art is under strict censorship so that no form of artistic expression may be used as a veiled attack on the principles of the new regime. The same holds of scientific research. Scientists who are not in full sympathy with the Soviet ideals are excluded from membership in academies of science, and from active participation in scientific research. Religion is treated even worse than art and science. Due partly to the close connection between organized religion and the old régime in Russia, and partly to the essentially materialistic and atheistic Marxian philosophy on which the Soviet State is based, every possible obstacle is placed in the way of the worshiper. As we have already indicated, the younger generation is being systematically taught atheism and encouraged not to practice religion. The Soviet schools and universities are for the most part propaganda institutions. The Soviet authorities are determined that no institutions shall develop that may rival the Soviet State in the esteem and interests of the people.

Yet culture is not dead in Russia. In fact the people are encouraged to enjoy music, drama, and other forms of art. Scientific research is subsidized by the Soviet State. Mr. Hanchin writes: "In the socialistic city of the future there will be a new culture. When we speak of a polytechnic education, we mean also a universal education. Of course, this does not mean that a person will be expected to know everything, but nothing thoroughly. A man will have his field of specialization, and he will also have a broad, general knowledge of every branch of modern culture. The words of the British naturalist, Huxley, 'To know something about everything and everything about something,' will be applicable to every member of the socialist community." [7]

Perhaps the greatest contribution of the Soviet State to culture has been the deliberate encouragement of the various separate cultures within the wide environs of Russia to develop in their own way. Each separate group is permitted to use its own language and to practice its own folk customs. This is a decided advance over the treatment accorded to the cultural minorities in the old Imperial Russia, and it is bound to lead to a great enrichment of culture in the end. Then, too, the Soviet authorities are not especially hostile to the purely cultural treasures of the old régime, and these will undoubtedly continue to form a part of the culture of the Russian people. This is especially true of prewar Russian literature and art. Thus the subordination of the cultural order to the Soviet State is probably purely temporary. In the end new cultural values will be created, and new cultural institutions will gain strength. Every revolution is harmful to culture temporarily, but when the new

[7] *Loco citato*, p. 29.

régime establishes itself firmly there is usually a great enhancement of cultural values. No doubt this will prove true in the Soviet State.

So we must conclude that the Soviet State represents an advance over the old Imperial Russia from an ethical point of view. More of the citizens of Russia have an opportunity for self-realization, and on the whole the Soviet State represents the real will of the Russian people far better than did the old régime. No doubt a foundation is being laid in Russia for the creation of a new type of representative democracy. Whether this will come about by gradual evolution or by a violent revolution, no one can predict. But compared with the governments of the free peoples of the western world the Soviet State is far from giving to its citizens what those governments are giving to their nationals. It has a long way to go before it attains what they have attained, however defective they may be when measured by our two sets of criteria. And one who believes in progress must believe that the Russian people will eventually achieve true freedom. But let us apply our two sets of criteria to Fascism and Nazism before dealing in detail with the free peoples of the world.

What to Read

The student will find the following books on the three leading Bolshevik dictators interesting and informative: *Lenin,* by D. S. Mirsky; *Stalin,* by S. Dmitrievsky; *Stalin* by Stephen Graham; *Stalin and the Red Army,* by K. Voroshilof (included in a symposium on Stalin, edited by Naganovitch); and *My Life* by Leon Trotsky.

Stalin's own writings entitled: *Leninism; Political Report to the 16th Party Congress;* and *Marxism and the National Question* are important sources, as are also M. Ilin's *New Russia Primer* and V. M. Molotof's two books: *The Five Year Plan,* and *The New Phase in the Soviet Union.* See also the *Bolshevik Documents,* pp. 269-359, of Waldemar Gurian's *Bolshevism: Theory and Practice* (translated from the German by E. I. Watkin). Gurian's book is an especially valuable critique of Bolshevism from our point of view, because he uses some of our criteria as a basis for his evaluation (see chs. III and VI). William Henry Chamberlin's *The Soviet Planned Economic Order* and *Russia's Iron Age,* and Samuel N. Harper's *Making Bolsheviks* and *Civic Training in Soviet Russia* are also especially informative.

For the general background of the political philosophy which has produced the Soviet State see especially F. W. Coker's *Recent Political Philosophy,* Pt. I, chs. II-VI, and the copious references given at the end of each chapter, and in particular the extensive bibliography on pp. 184-191. See also Harry W. Laidler: *Socialism in Thought and Action,* and *A History of Socialist Thought;* and Arthur Rosenberg: *A History of Bolshevism.* The classic works of Karl Marx that are available in English are: *Poverty of Philosophy; The Communist Manifesto; The Class Struggles in France; A Contribution to the Critique of Political Economy; Value, Price, and Profit; The Civil War in France; The Gotha Program;* and, most important of all, *Capital: a Critique of Political Economy.* Compare S. H. M. Chang: *The Marxian Theory of the State.*

Some other good books on Russia for the general reader

are: Michael T. Florinsky: *World Revolution and the U. S. S. R.;* Maurice Hindus: *Humanity Uprooted; Broken Earth; Red Bread;* and *The Great Offensive;* Bruce Hopper: *Pan-Sovietism;* Alexander Kerensky: *The Crucifixion of Liberty;* H. J. Laski: *Communism;* Allan Monkhouse: *Moscow, 1911-1933;* Bertrand Russell: *Bolshevism: Practice and Theory;* Jessica Smith: *Woman in Soviet Russia.* See also the books cited in the footnotes of this chapter.

CHAPTER VI

CONFORMITY OF ACTUAL STATES TO THE IDEAL: DICTATORSHIPS

1. Extent and Uniqueness of Contemporary Dictatorships

Referring again to Professor MacIver's classification of states (see the table on pp. 83 f.), we find that he classified dynastic or oligarchic states under Division IV on the basis of the derivation of the power wielded by the actual sovereign. This division was divided into three main types of states: hereditary, elective, and dictatorial. As a matter of fact all three are dictatorial in the broad sense of the word, since an hereditary oligarchy is a dictatorship of an absolute monarch who obtained his power by inheritance, and an elective oligarchy is one in which the supreme potentate secured his power by election, whereas the dictatorial type is one in which the ruler obtained control by the use of force. But regardless of how they derive their power all three types of sovereigns are actual dictators after they get it and in the exercise of it. In this chapter we shall attempt to apply the postulates and three orders of an ideal state to dictatorships, howsoever the dictator may have secured his power over the people he governs.

No postwar political phenomenon is any more noteworthy than the rapid expansion of the dictatorial principle in government. When the Versailles Treaty was finally completed nearly every country of Western Europe had a parliamentary government of a democratic type. Even those who were ruled by an hereditary monarch were organized as representative democracies. This condition turned out to be one of unstable equilibrium. As a result of the ravages of the World War the internal affairs of many of these states were in such a chaotic condition that the people were unable to function politically. Many of them lost their hard-won rights to govern themselves. Representative democracies were replaced by dictatorships as tyrannical as ever have been known in West European history. At present this type of government is strongly entrenched in Italy, Germany, Poland, Jugoslavia, Austria, Bulgaria, Turkey, and in a number of other small countries of the Eastern and Western hemispheres.

Moreover, at least the two largest and most important of these dictatorships are in many respects unique, namely, Fascism and Nazism. Their uniqueness consists in the fact that they are nationalistic-socialistic states, in which concentration of authority in a supreme ruler is accompanied by a complete socialization of industry within the borders of the state. Thus Fascism under Mussolini has created the "corporative state" and Hitler has created what has been called "the state of estates." In both cases there is virtually a complete socialization of all industry. Because of this uniqueness defenders of these two leading forms of contemporary dictatorships argue that they represent a distinct advance over the so-called liberal bourgeoise type of state. We are thus confronted with the insistent claim that a new type of state has arisen which makes representative democracy obsolete.

In making this claim defenders of Fascism and Nazism are like defenders of Sovietism in being devided into two groups. One group maintains that the liberal democratic state is inferior to Fascism so far as the Italian people are concerned, and inferior to Nazism so far as the German people are concerned. They hold that conditions within Italy and within Germany were such that these dictatorships were the only hope. Had they not arisen, both countries would have made an abject surrender to Russian communism, and would have become Soviet States. The other group argues that the fascist principle is superior to the principle of democracy for all peoples of the earth, and that the fascist type of government will ultimately supplant democracy everywhere, since the liberal democratic state is "in itself a fragile structure." This difference is important theoretically but not practically, since both groups are chiefly interested in consolidating the dictatorial governments in those places where they have become actual. But it is most significant and ominous that some intelligent citizens of democratic governments, especially in France, England, and the United States, are of the opinion that democracy is obsolete, and that it will ultimately be replaced as a form of government either by the soviet or by the fascist principle.

2. Difficulty of Applying the Postulates and Three Orders to Dictatorships

In approaching the task of applying our four postulates of an ideal state and our three orders to dictatorships we are faced again with a serious difficulty. For our ideal state was set up on the basic assumption that the welfare and development of its citizens is the moral purpose and the *raison d'être* of every political state. We argued that men and women and children are faced with the problem of realizing themselves, as fully as possible, that the end and meaning of their existence is to exercise all of their specifically human capacities, and that the state has arisen because individuals found it necessary to coöperate in meeting the three kinds of evils which confront them, and has evolved naturally out of more primitive forms of social organization, as people have become more and more conscious of their needs and of what would satisfy those needs. In the words of John Dewey, and the pragmatist philosophers generally, there exists a hyphenated trinity: *need-demand-satisfaction*, and this is the natural basis of all social organization. States exist only because men find it easier to meet the needs and demands of intelligent living by cooperating through the state and its numerous institutions. This assumption of the subordination of the state to the satisfaction of human needs is basic to our conception of the ideal state.

The dictatorships absolutely deny this assumption. They proclaim the principle that individuals and groups must sacrifice themselves in the interest of the political solidarity of the people occupying a certain territory. This has been well expressed by Alfred Rocco, Minister of Justice under Mussolini. He writes: "The individual cannot be considered as the ultimate end of society. Society has its own purposes of preservation, expansion and perfection, and these are distinct from the purposes of the individuals who at any one moment compose it. In the carrying out of its own proper ends, society must make use of individuals. This entirely reverses the expressive formula of Immanuel Kant, 'the individual is the end and cannot be considered as the means to the end.' The State, however, which is the legal organization of society, is for Fascism an organism distinct from the citizens who at any given time form part of it; it has its own life and its own superior ends, to which the ends of the individual must be subordinated. . . . And since the State must realize its own ends, which are superior to those of the individual, it must also have superior and more powerful resources. The force of the State must exceed every other force; that is to say, the State must be absolutely sovereign and must dominate all the existing forces in the country, coordinate them, solidify them, and direct them towards the higher ends of national life." [1]

Such an appeal to the principle of sacrificing human beings for the good of the state shows how far the dictatorships go in rejecting the fundamental principle of the political ethics hitherto dominant in the western world. The Kantian principle referred to by Minister Rocco is one of the forms of his famous categorical imperative or moral law: "So act as to treat humanity, whether in thine own person or in that of any other, in every case as an end withal, never as means only," and it is deliberately rejected. The state has the right to use its citizens as means to the realization of its august ends. Obviously it is difficult to apply postulates, based upon the assumption that persons are to be treated as ends and never as means, to an actual state which deliberately rejects that assumption, and builds upon its opposite.

It may be freely admitted that every individual should be willing to sacrifice himself for the state whenever the state's existence is threatened, since its destruction deprives him and his posterity of the essential means of self-realization. Consequently, the state always has the right to call upon its citizens for military service, as well as for other forms of public service. And in cases of necessity it has the right to compel such service. We are not ques-

[1] See *What is Fascism and Why?* Edited by Tomaso Sillani, Ernest Benn, London, 1931, p. 18.

tioning these rights that are a part of the very conception of the liberal democratic state. We are merely pointing out that dictatorships are built on the principle that the necessity for the compulsion of citizens always exists. *They have erected an emergency principle into a permanent principle.* Instead of stating the relation of the state to the individual as it is normally they have stated that relation as it is in a time of national crisis. But national crises pass and with them go the governments that a people create to deal with them. Dictatorships are emergency forms of government and they live by keeping emergencies alive. They appeal to the baser elements in human nature: fear and the spirit of revenge and hate.

3. Application of the Four Postulates to Dictatorships

(a) *The Postulate of Identical Ideals.*—According to this postulate an ideal social order is one in which there is an identity between what individuals wish to make out of themselves, and what others or the state wishes to make of them. Under dictatorships there is an apparent conformity to this postulate. The youth do seem to share the ideals of the dictator. This is true of the young people of both Italy and Germany. There is an organized body of youth under each régime, and these youth movements constitute one of the main elements of strength of the Hitler and Mussolini governments. A recent intelligent observer, after several months on the continent of Europe, Dr. Stephen Duggan, Director of the Institute of International Education, says: "There are many causes for the enthusiasm of youth in the dictatorship countries. Youth is emphatically the period of emotional appeal, especially patriotic appeal. As the result of education and propaganda, young Italians feel they were shabbily treated at Versailles and young Germans that they were outrageously treated at Versailles. . . . Moreover, the youth of these countries, whether students or workers, have been without prospects since the war. The democratic régimes seemed to provide no future. The dictatorship promised better things. Patriotism and personal interest combined to make a stirring appeal which has met with an enthusiastic response.

"It is difficult to visit the democratic countries without realizing a considerable lack of enthusiasm for democracy among the youth. While there is no danger of revolution in France, French youth regard the present parliamentary régime with contempt. And in both England and the United States there is a good deal of cynicism among the youth of our colleges concerning democratic institutions." [2] Obviously the young people of Germany and Italy have a much greater enthusiasm for the dictatorial régimes under which they live than American young people have for democracy. So the postulate of identical ideals does seem to be met.

[2] *News Bulletin of the Institute of International Education*, Vol. 9, No. 8, p. 3.

DICTATORSHIPS

Nevertheless when we raise the question of how this identity is secured grave doubts arise as to its genuineness. For it is not through the mechanism of the anatomy of admiration, by means of which a youth is able to form an ideal for himself by synthesizing those elements in the interested and disinterested ideals that are offered to him by his parents and various recommenders, that this identity is secured under dictatorships. It is by a rigid control of education through which the kind of an ideal for youth that the dictator wishes is imposed upon all young people. Every youth, from a very early age, is under the strictest supervision of Nazi or Fascist party representatives. He is thoroughly indoctrinated into the principles of the dictatorship under which he lives. All the devices of propaganda known to influence youth are employed in the process of producing a deathless enthusiasm and reverence for the supreme head of the party and of the government. Mussolini and Hitler are all but worshipped by organized masses of young people. No ideal is countenanced which is incompatible in any way with the inculcation of devotion to the leader. Hence the identity of ideals is not such as may exist among a free people where all sorts of ideals are held up before youth so that each one may select for himself the kind of a career he desires to follow. It is an identity forced on youth by a deliberate propaganda policy, and not an identity developed internally according to the laws of psychical growth and moral development. It is a blind and abject form of hero worship.

(b) *The Postulate of the Transformation of Competitive Into Non-Competitive Interests.*—Do dictatorships offer to their citizens an adequate opportunity to transform the mere love of money and of the power that money gives into an abiding interest in cultural values? Here again, the highly socialistic character of the two leading contemporary dictatorships gives one the impression that they conform to the requirements of this postulate. Every aspect of the economic life is rigidly controlled. Capital, management, labor, and consumption are completely regimented. The state practically determines what the owner and manager receive as net profit and salary, what the wages for each industry shall be, and the price paid by consumers. In Mussolini's "corporative state" as well as in Hitler's "state of estates" the entire economic life of the people, down to the minutest details, is so regulated as to give to the state practically all the increment that accrues. So far as the individual is concerned, competition is certainly transformed under these régimes, but again, not by individuals learning from their own experience that the power of ideas is far greater than the power of wealth, but by the state taking over all of the fruits of industry. The result is that the cultural values are completely subordinated to the ends of the state.

(c) *The Postulates of Constructive Criticism and of Conserving Force.*—Do dictatorships encourage the maintenance of a balance between criticism and conservation, so far as the institutions making up the state are concerned? By no means. No criticism is tolerated. People are fined and even imprisoned for making some chance remark that can be interpreted as derogatory of Hitler or Mussolini. After the death of President von Hindenberg, Hitler required every man in the German army to take an oath of personal allegiance to him. And in spite of the fact that his own book, *Mein Kampf,* is filled with the most fanatical kind of criticism, in his Hamburg speech in August, 1934, Herr Hitler denounced criticism and said that he considered it to have no value. Freedom of speech is completely destroyed as a matter of principle. On the other hand, all kinds of propaganda are indulged in to strengthen the régime with the people. In Germany the Nazi and in Italy the Fascist party alone is recognized. Each party is in complete control of and is an integral part of the government. There is no opposition party. None is permitted. As a result the balance between constructive criticism and conserving power is completely upset. Under such conditions the evils in institutions are sure to multiply and to become increasingly more burdensome to the people.

Thus the dictatorships have to be condemned as not meeting adequately the requirements of any of the four postulates, howsoever much they may appear to conform to them. The claim that these régimes mark a step forward in social organization is not well founded. In fact, it is false, and its opposite is true. Judged by the four postulates of an ideal state, Nazism and Fascism are undoubtedly retrogressive movements.

4. APPLICATION OF THE THREE ORDERS TO DICTATORSHIPS

What, now, is the condition of the three orders of an ideal society in the countries under dictators? First, let us consider the *private order,* and especially its chief institution, the family.

There can be no doubt that the dictators are seriously interested in the strengthening of the family. Various laws and edicts have been issued both in Italy and in Germany, the sole purpose of which is to strengthen the family. Mothers' pensions, marriage bonuses, bachelor taxes, permanent peasant ownership of the land, family wage systems, and similar measures in support of the family have been put into effect. There is every evidence that both Hitler and Mussolini are impressed with the importance of the family as an institution, and that both of them regard it as the main bulwark of the state.

On the other hand, the lot of women has undoubtedly been made much harder under Nazism and Fascism. In Germany restrictive edicts against women entering the universities have been issued. Only ten per cent of those enrolled can be women. Likewise in Italy women are much worse off than they were under the former liberal government which preceded "the march on Rome." It is a significant fact that women who are citizens of representative democracies have formed an international organization to combat the restrictive measures against women which are in effect in Germany and in Italy. However, in Turkey, women are undoubtedly better off now than formerly. In fact, one can almost speak of the emancipation of women in Turkey under the dictatorship. However, on the whole, dictators are all opposed to the idea that women should have an opportunity to participate in the public order. Their philosophy of women's rights is summed up in the famous maxim: "Woman's place is in the home."

As we have already indicated, the dictators make the state the dominant institution of the public order and completely subordinate all of the aspects of the economic life to the state. No longer is the state treated as an instrument for the furthering of the cultural values. The cultural order is as much subordinated to the state as is the economic life. In Italy a serious conflict has arisen between Mussolini and the Pope over the treatment of youth, and especially over Mussolini's attempt to destroy the organization of young people formed by the Church. And in Germany a sharp conflict still rages over the attempt to control the Church by making Nazi ministers and bishops supreme. The inevitable tendency of the dictatorships is to make religion completely subservient to the state. And the same holds with respect to science and art. Liberal professors have been greatly restricted in Germany. Many of her great Jewish scientists and artists have been driven out of the country and their property confiscated. But the opposition to culture is not confined to cultured Jews. Hitler blames the intelligentsia for their cowardice and lack of enthusiasm in the World War and his policies are directly opposed to the cultural class in Germany. Just recently he has ordered a reduction of fifty per cent in the number who are allowed to attend the universities, and he has made the approval of the Nazi party an essential entrance requirement to a university. Unless the student's diploma for his college preparatory work has stamped upon it "patriotic merit" he cannot matriculate in any university. And Fascism is also neglecting the cultural order. Writing in *Current History* Hugh Quigley says: "Fascism's record of public service, particularly in the smaller towns and in the suburbs of the cities—public service as represented not only by utilities, but by such things as hospitals, sanataria and schools—is poorer than that of any other European country, and is certainly poorer than that of pre-Fascist Italy." (See Vol. XL, p. 258)

Yet it must be admitted that Mussolini has been more friendly to culture on the whole than has Hitler. For he has evidently finally settled the Vatican controversy and this has done a great deal to unify the Italian people religiously. However, on the whole, the dictatorships are advocates of the principle of the totalitarian state, and this means the complete subordination of the cultural order to the political.

5. General Conclusions

Our first conclusion must be that the dictatorships do not adequately meet the three evils inherent in any type of social order. They do not eliminate the clash between what an individual wishes to make out of himself and what the state wishes to make out of him. They simply do violence to all individual initiative in the formation of ideals and impose their own ideal. They do not deal adequately with the evils inherent in the very nature of competitive values, but merely despoil their citizens in the promotion of military and other governmental schemes. They do not eliminate the evils in institutions by providing for their gradual improvement by the process of free criticism. On the contrary, these evils are bound to increase through the years due to the absence of the necessary corrective measures. Dictatorships are governments that lack the mechanisms that are essential to the permanent alleviation of human misery arising from the three kinds of evils.

Then, too, there is a peculiar paradox which the dictators will not be able to meet. The present dictators attained their own self-realization and development under liberal régimes where they were allowed a freedom which they deny to others. They became dictators because the people, over whom they now exercise control, permitted them to grow from childhood to manhood under a liberal and parliamentary government. But the children who are now growing to manhood under their dictatorships are not allowed to develop the way they were permitted to realize themselves. Whence, then, are to come the leaders who must eventually succeed them? The system does not develop the type of leadership which these dictators exemplify. They were created under another system. Time will prove the need for leaders who have sufficient character and intelligence to perpetuate their régimes, but their régimes do not produce that kind of leaders.

This paradox is more far-reaching than has just been indicated. Not only do the dictatorships prevent the training of real political leaders and farsighted statesmen, but they actually produce by their system of education a type of mass mentality which works against creativity. Under a régime where economic freedom, political liberty, academic freedom, and freedom of conscience and of speech are regarded as vices, a subservient type of mentality will inevitably result. People will practice hypocrisy and cunning and will subvert the plans of the authorities by deceitful practices. And this will lower the general level of culture.

Dean Roscoe Pound has said that the fundamental principle of stability in a social order is the maintenance of a technique of change. He means that a government cannot be durable and stable unless its administrators allow for unforeseen changes which time is sure to bring to every people. The dictatorships have no such technique and the system of government which they exemplify is incapable of providing such a technique. In the end they will not be able to cope with future contingencies. All of their policies place them in the predicament of having either to expand or to explode. They deliberately encourage an increase in population in order to strengthen their military power. Their own territories will not support this excess population. Hemmed in by free peoples their efforts to expand will be met by a resistance unto death on the part of these free peoples. Thus their problems will multiply. They will be destroyed by internal combustion or by the power of the free peoples whom they cannot enslave. The mills of the gods grind slowly but they grind exceeding fine. And history proves that every government by a dictator ultimately has been ground to powder. And there is no evidence to indicate that Fascism and Nazism, or any of the other dictatorships now extant on the earth, will be able to escape the relentless forces that are already at work to destroy them.

Our judgment of Nazism and Fascism must be harsher than our judgment of Sovietism, even though this is not the view of many. For Sovietism recognizes the instrumental character of the state, even predicting a type of human social organization in which there will be no state, whereas Nazism and Fascism are ultra-fanatical in their worship of the state. Then, too, Sovietism is a step forward in Russia from a type of despotism that was worse than it is, whereas Nazism and Fascism are retrogressive movements which have robbed peoples that formerly enjoyed liberal governmental institutions of the freedom that once was theirs. Sovietism can develop into something better and is evidently on the road to doing so. Nazism and Facism are dragging their people down into a condition of permanent subservience. Sovietism is producing a higher culture in Russia to replace the lower decadent culture of the czars. Nazism and Facism must make way for liberty, if the rich cultures of Germany and Italy are to be conserved and enhanced.

Nevertheless, let us not deceive ourselves. For in choosing between Russian Communism and Fascism we are choosing between two evils. Any government which robs its citizens of liberty and deprives them of a knowledge of the truth must be condemned. No such governments can satisfy the deepest needs of human beings. Based upon the principle that might makes right in dealing with their own citizens, these governments are essentially unethical. We concur fully with Mr. Chester Rowell: "Every Communist or Fascist dictatorship on earth today makes the suppression of truth the very first article of its policy. It abolishes liberty of speech and of the press; it propagandizes education, and turns research from the scientific quest of truth to its own ends. Even history is distorted into fiction; economic study is regimented; art is prostituted; scholarship is neither free nor fruitful;

science is the handmaiden of politics; and teaching, speaking, preaching, writing, and printing are all under orders. That way lies the death of human progress." And he is certainly right when he says: "The ages when Truth was suppressed were the ages when everything else stagnated and finally retrograded." [3] Modern dictators cannot long survive the assault they have deliberately made upon the citadel of truth. Men may be enslaved but truth can never be. In the end the hard facts against which the dictators kick will furnish the poisonous pricks to pierce their Achilles heel.

This conclusion is so overwhelmingly important to every person enjoying the benefits of citizenship in a representative democracy that it should be clinched still further with positive and irrefutable proof. After spending eight months visiting representatives of the Institute of International Education in Europe, Dr. Stephan Duggan, Secretary of the Institute, wrote:

"Where do economic security and economic freedom exist? In dictatorship countries? Certainly not. In every dictatorship the individual is subject to absolute control by the state. Wherever political liberty has been destroyed, there economic freedom is dead. The status of the working people in practically every European country was gradually raised as a result of their being organized into trade unions which could defend their interests. In every

[3] Quoted from the *San Francisco Chronicle* in the *American Observer*, Vol. III, p. 4.

country where there has been a Fascist revolution the trade unions have been destroyed and despite the promises of dictatorships, whether individual or group, to safeguard the interests of the workers, those interests have been sacrificed whenever the dictatorship has considered it necessary and there remained no organization to defend them. Moreover, the right of the manufacturer to act by himself or through groups is very strictly limited or controlled by the government as a necessary result of a dictatorship. . . . No mistake should be made by the intellectual classes as to their economic status under dictatorships. Through government control over all jobs no teacher can hold his place a moment unless he teaches the right doctrine. His economic security and economic freedom die at once. Through the control over the economic position of the teacher there is established practically complete restraint over his intellectual freedom. The government regulates his intellectual freedom by its control over the printing press and by its refusing to allow him to publish writings not in harmony with its theories. Finally, the government has the prison and the concentration camp at its disposal so that it is fair to say that the door of intellectual freedom is triple locked in dictatorship countries.

"I have taken the fate of the teacher as typical of what happens to the intellectual in general. The tomb-like stillness that has settled upon such splendid former organs of public opinion as the *Corriera della Sera* of Milan, the *Neue Freie Presse* of

Vienna or the *Frankfurter Zeitung* when confronted with momentous public problems that demand solutions that may be opposed to those of the dictatorship is eloquent of what has happened to the journalist and the publicist.

"This appeal is directed only to Americans. Other peoples have a right to decide their own forms of government. But American workers, manual and intellectual, should not forget that there is an indissoluble connection between political liberty and economic freedom, that the former is the precursor of the latter, and that despite the defects of democracy, it is only in a democracy that to any extent political liberty and economic freedom have found existence." [4]

These words of a competent and informed thinker should put to rest the vain fancyings of any free citizen that he would be better off under a dictatorship. The truth is that such fancies are usually due to the fact that those who dream them imagine themselves to be the dictator or, at least, one of his advisers! But when the blind lead the blind all fall into the same pit.

What to Read

Three works of Benito Mussolini are available in English: *My Autobiography; The Political and Social Doctrine of Fascism,* translated by Jane Soames and published in the *Political Quarterly,* Vol. IV, pp. 341-356; *Mussolini as Revealed in His Political Speeches,* translated and edited by

[4] *News Bulletin of the Institute,* Vol. X, No. 1, p. 3 (Oct. 1934).

Bernardo Quaranta di San Severino. Adolf Hitler's *My Battle* has been translated into English with approximately 160,000 words omitted. See the article *Hitler Unexpurgated: Deletions from "Mein Kampf"* by Miriam Beard in the volume entitled: *Nazism: An Assault on Civilization*, edited by Pierre Van Paassen and James Waterman Wise, a volume containing other good articles on Nazism. See Emil Lengyel: *Hitler*.

Other valuable discussions of Fascism are the following: the articles entitled: *Fascism*, and *Fascism, Economics of*, in the 14th edition of the *Encyclopedia Britannica;* Ivanoe Bonomi: *From Socialism to Fascism: a Study of Contemporary Italy;* F. L. Benns: *Europe Since 1914* (Revised Edition); Raymond Leslie Buell: *Europe: A History of Ten Years;* F. W. Coker: *Recent Political Thought*, Ch. XVII (contains a valuable bibliography, pp. 492-496); W. Y. Elliott: *The Pragmatic Revolt in Politics*, Ch. XI; Otto Forst-Battaglia, editor: *Dictatorship on Trial*, translated by Huntley Paterson; Giovanni Gentile: *The Philosophical Basis of Fascism* in *Foreign Affairs*, Vol. VI, pp. 290-304. G. M. Godden: *Mussolini: The Birth of the New Democracy;* Francesco S. Nitti: *Bolshevism, Fascism, and Democracy*, translated by Margaret M. Green; Alberto Pennachio: *The Corporative State;* Odon Por: *Fascism*, translated by E. Townshend; Giuseppe Prezzolini: *Fascism*, translated by Kathleen Macmillan; Alfredo Rocco: *The Political Doctrines of Fascism;* Herbert W. Schneider: *Making the Fascist State* (contains important source material, pp. 257-363, and a valuable bibliography, pp. 365-385); Thomaso Sillani, editor: *What is Fascism and Why?;* Suigi Villari: *The Fascist Experiment* and *Italy;* John Strachey: *The Menace of Fascism*.

Some good books on Nazism are the following: H. F.

Armstrong: *Hitler's Reich: The First Phase;* Raymond Leslie Buell, editor: *New Governments in Europe;* Everett R. Clinchey: *The Strange Case of Herr Hitler;* Calvin B. Hoover: *Germany Enters the Third Reich;* Paul Kosol: *Modern Germany: a Study of Conflicting Loyalties;* Helmut Klotz: *The Berlin Diaries: May 30, 1932-Jan. 30, 1933;* Heinz Liepmann: *Murder: Made in Germany;* Willi Muenzenberg: *The Brown Book of the Hitler Terror;* Nordicas(pseud.): *Hitlerism: the Iron Fist in Germany;* Oswald Garrison Villard: *The German Phoenix.*

For the general background of German political and economic conditions out of which Nazism emerged see Moeller van den Bruck: *Germany's Third Empire,* and for a recent explanation and interpretation of the movement see George Nolin: *Hitlerism—Why and Whither* in Bulletins of University of Colorado, Vol. XXXIV, No. 7, March 29, 1934.

Since Nazism is so recent I add a list of good magazine articles: Miriam Beard: "The Nazis Harness Woman Power" in *Today* May 12, 1934; Sidney B. Fay: "The Nazi 'Totalitarian' State," *Current History,* August, 1933, pp. 610-618; Harold D. Lasswell: "The Psychology of Hitlerism," *Political Quarterly,* Vol. IV, pp. 373-384; Raymond Moley: "Hitlerism: Enemy of the Christian Church" in *Today,* April 21, 1934; F. W. von Prittwitz: "Germany in Transition," *Current History,* Vol. XXXVIII, pp. 385-391; Otto D. Tolischus: "Hitler's Industrial Utopia: The State of Estates Plan," *New York Times,* July 23, 1933; Leon Trotsky: "What Hitler Wants" in *Harper's Magazine,* Sept., 1933; Mildred S. Wertheimer: "Forces Underlying the Nazi Revolution" in *Foreign Policy Reports,* Vol. IX, No. 10 (July 19, 1933). The economic crisis in Germany is well presented in two articles by R. S. Ocker and

R. C. Long in *Current History,* Vol. XL, pp. 425-430 and pp. 651-657.

See also the popular articles: "Old Time Germany Looks at Hitler" by F. Britten Austin in the *Saturday Evening Post,* August 5, 1933, and "Let Napoleon Do It" by Eugene Lyons in the *Cosmopolitan,* August, 1934.

CHAPTER VII

CONFORMITY OF ACTUAL STATES TO THE IDEAL: REPRESENTATIVE DEMOCRACIES

1. The Extent and Importance of Representative Democracies

Referring once more to Professor MacIver's classification of the forms of states, we find that he distinguishes first between the unitary and composite forms of democracy on the basis of external structure, and between direct unitary democracy and representative unitary democracy, with the latter subdivided into the limited monarchy and the republic on the basis of whether there is a titular monarch or an elected president. These subdivisions are useful in showing that the term representative democracy is broad enough to cover a rather large variety of actually existing states. It is a serious mistake to suppose that a government is not democratic unless the monarch is an elected official, limited to one or more short terms of office. Yet it is a mistake that many people make.

Using the term representative democracy in the broad sense which we have just indicated, it is important to stress the fact that states having this form of government are still numerous and among the most powerful on earth; since there are some writers and speakers who infer that the reaction against democracy is already everywhere dominant, and that it will soon overwhelm the few democracies that are left. This inference is entirely fallacious. All countries of an Anglo-Saxon origin must be numbered among the representative democracies that are still extant. These include the United States of America, Great Britain, and the nations making up with Great Britain what is usually called the British Commonwealth of Nations—that is, the self-governing dominions such as Canada, Australia, and New Zealand. To these must be added all of the progressive and enlightened self-governing states of northwestern Europe: Sweden, Norway, Denmark, Holland, and Belgium. There is also France, which remains the greatest representative democracy on the continent of Europe, and in addition Switzerland, Czechoslovakia, and some small countries in the Balkan peninsula, around the Baltic Sea, and in Central and South America, where free institutions still abide and function for the welfare of millions of the most progressive peoples on earth. The fact is that all of these countries, together with their dependencies, constitute a majority of the civilized people of the earth.

Representative democracies achieved their greatest expansion immediately following the World War, when for a time the Central Powers, the Balkan States, and Italy, all of which are now under dictatorships, were numbered among the free

REPRESENTATIVE DEMOCRACIES

peoples of the world. Although democracy has lost a number of countries in which it was temporarily established we should not count this to the discredit of this form of government. As Sir Herbert Samuel has well stated in an article in *Current History:* "Among the states in which liberty has been overthrown are several where it has never been long or firmly established. No one would regard Russia or Poland, Turkey or Persia, as lands of historic freedom. It is more remarkable that for brief spells parliamentary institutions should have been established there than that they should have soon disappeared." (See Vol. XL, p. 266) Critics of democracy, who regard it as a "fragile structure," also admit that it is too deeply rooted among many peoples to be replaced by fascist or communistic principles. Thus the Italian Minister of Justice, Alfred Rocco, writes: "Outside Italy, and especially in Anglo-Saxon countries, the liberal-democratic State has been able to flourish and to achieve great results, because in the social and political conditions of those peoples it found correctives which we do not have. In the Anglo-Saxon countries, and also in France, there is a great national tradition, and the idea of the State has been fortified by centuries of struggle maintained by the State to affirm its own supremacy. Besides, in England the individualistic and disintegratory spirit of Germanism is counteracted by a rigorous moral education, so that the individual, while theoretically maintaining perfect liberty in the face of the State, knows of himself how to keep it within limits."[1] Severe as is the economic depression, there is really no serious danger of any people that has been long schooled in self-government ever surrendering to any form of dictatorship.

If there were a union today of all the free peoples of the world, so constituted as to make it possible for them to wield their combined strength as one people, they could easily destroy or subjugate every government on earth that is based on undemocratic principles. For the free peoples have an overwhelming superiority in military equipment and in trained army and navy personnel, the most of the wealth of the earth, and the highest developed technology, to say nothing of the fact that those portions of the earth which they occupy are especially favored from the standpoint of climate and other geographic factors. Moreover, the success of the Soviet leaders in Russia, as well as that of leaders in many other lands, has been very largely due to the guidance they have received from a host of experts who were trained in and by the institutions of the free peoples of the earth. All of this needs to be emphasized because it is so often overlooked by superficial propagandists, who are desirous of undermining democracy and of replacing it with Fascism or Communism. Representative democracy, taken in its entirety, must be admitted to be the most powerful form of government existing on the earth today. Those peoples who are enjoying the highest standard of living ever attained by human beings

[1] *Loco citato*, p. 17.

REPRESENTATIVE DEMOCRACIES

all live under democracies. No other form of government has been able to give as much to its citizens as has this form. This is an incontrovertible fact and not a mere opinion. And it is a fact of which the bitterest enemies of democracy are fully aware. Indeed it is one of the causes of their enmity.

2. APPLICATION OF THE FOUR POSTULATES TO REPRESENTATIVE DEMOCRACIES

(a) *The Postulate of Identical Ideals.*—In all free countries children are so exposed to such a variety of interested and disinterested ideals that they are able to form for themselves an ideal of what they wish to make out of themselves. And on the whole, they are permitted to spend their energies in the realization of that ideal. And not only are they permitted to do so, they are aided by their government, as children, as well as when they reach maturity, in innumerable ways. They may patent their inventions, copyright their books and other literary creations, they may incorporate their business, obtain governmental or other aid in almost any kind of research, all because representative democracies are operated on the principle that the human values are the highest values. Such governments seek to develop their citizens and they recognize that this is their chief function.

The weakness of democracies is their tendency towards paternalism and bureaucracy. They do too much, not too little, for the promotion of the welfare of their members. The result is that many young people grow up with no enthusiasm for the ideal of democracy itself. They are like King Lear's daughters, who turned him out into the storm after he gave them all he had. And, like King Lear, a democracy sometimes finds it necessary to heap curses upon the head of many an ungrateful citizen who turns into a grafter or criminal, so that they may

> Feel how like a serpent's tooth it is
> To have a thankless child.

We provide free public education for our children, and some of them spend their energies in riotous living through the long hours of the night, thereby incapacitating themselves for the self-improvement which the educational systems place within their reach. We supply our children with free textbooks, and many of them proceed to deface and to defile what was placed in their hands for their enlightenment. We must find a way to stimulate our young people to form for themselves worthy ideals and to seek to realize them. We must avoid pampering them and making them think that the world owes them a living. We must make them love democracy more than an Italian loves Mussolini, or a German loves Hitler, or a Russian loves Stalin.

(b) *The Postulate of the Transformation of Competitive Into Non-Competitive Interests.*—Do democracies make it possible for large numbers of their citizens to transform their acquisitive instinct, and other competitive interests into an interest in truth for truth's sake, and an interest in art for art's sake? Do we teach our children to love wealth for the power it gives over others or for the power it gives to help others? Do we stress the accumulation of hordes of gold and of other economic goods, or do we rather emphasize the appreciation of the cultural values represented by science, religion, and the fine arts? Undoubtedly democracies do a great deal to foster culture and to make the cultural values available for all of their citizens. They maintain museums and libraries, they foster learned societies and research laboratories, and they issue innumerable pamphlets and monographs free of all charge in order that culture may be as widely disseminated as possible. Much is done by every democracy to impress its citizens with the importance and value of using their economic goods for the attainment of cultural ends for themselves and for their children.

However, no democracy ever has succeeded in preventing the struggle for economic goods from becoming a game of grab. None has succeeded in preventing the concentration of wealth in the hands of a relatively few people, while millions of the population lack enough to live decently, to say nothing of developing their cultural interests. The greatest weakness in democracies is to be found in their failure adequately to provide for the fulfilment of the requirements of this postulate. A way must be found to provide an equality of opportunity for self-realization on the part of every citizen. If this is not done, democracy is in real danger of being replaced by some other form of government. The rich and privileged classes must cease despoiling the under-privileged groups. All the children of every community must be given adequate training to equip them for full participation in the life of the state.

(c) *The Postulates of Constructive Criticism and Conserving Force.*—The extent to which the citizens of a country are allowed to criticise its institutions is perhaps the easiest way to determine whether they are a free people. In Hyde Park, London, one will find all kinds of soap-box orators expressing their opinions on almost every topic under the sun. They are free to say what they think. And in every democracy the rights to free speech, to freedom of conscience, to a free press, to academic freedom, to freedom of worship are recognized as inalienable rights, and as corollaries of the general right to liberty. A people which safeguards these rights is a free people, whereas a people that surrenders them is an enslaved people. And those who fully appreciate the value of the many institutions of a democracy are also free to meet the criticism with a conserving force that is proportionate to their certainty. Those two postulates are most adequately met in representative democracies.

Today the citizens of all democracies must ever be on their guard against the hidden control and subtle manipulation of all of the means of expressing public opinion. They must give careful heed to the wise words of Walt Whitman:

> I say that there can be no salvation for these States without innovators, without free tongues, and ears willing to hear the tongues,
> And I announce as a glory of these States that they respectfully listen to propositions, reforms, fresh views and doctrines.

There are innumerable devices for turning a free press into a controlled press. It is rumored that some college professors and high school teachers are occasionally subservient to various interests. War-time propaganda was so successful that numerous blocs and special privilege groups have been indulging in it vigorously ever since. And this threatens the proper functioning of the mechanisms presupposed by the postulates of constructive criticism and conserving force. Nevertheless, these postulates are unquestionably still functioning in all representative democracies, and they are effectively meeting the evils that arise from the fixity and rigidity of institutions.

3. Application of the Three Orders to Representative Democracies

Every democracy maintains the institutions of the *private order* and makes the family life central in that order. A great deal is done to protect the family and to prevent the disintegration of home life. The leaders of democracies recognize the value of home ownership and of decent housing conditions. They know that the chief source of human happiness is in those intimate relationships of life which find their highest expression in the family.

It is among the free peoples of the earth that sports and all forms of play have attained their highest development. It is a noteworthy fact that a large majority of the participants in the Olympic Games are citizens of representative democracies. No other people have succeeded so well in teaching their citizens the value of play, or have developed to so great an extent the organized institutions which provide for wholesome enjoyment and amusement, and for healthy exercise.

In connection with the private order it should also be especially pointed out that women have attained the greatest liberty under democratic governments. There are no dictatorships on earth today in which the lot of women is comparable with their status in representative democracies. It is under the democratic governments that home economics has become a science. Only the free peoples of the earth have succeeded in emancipating women from the drudgery of housekeeping, and in giving them the amount of leisure essential to self-cultivation and to participating in the public order. Hence, in general, the women citizens of free countries are noticeably superior to the women citizens of other lands; not natively superior, but superior in their attainments.

Nevertheless, these advantages carry with them certain evils which democracies must find a way to meet. There is a danger that the play institutions of the private order will become more important than the family. The emancipation of women from household drudgery carries with it an increasing reluctance to bear and to rear children. The interest women have in using their leisure for personal enjoyment and play conflicts with their duty to maintain the family on a basis where it can function in replenishing the race and in recreating its members. There are too many marriages for convenience and there are too many divorces in the families of the élite. Our amusements are too often merely distracting, if not positively harmful. They are not genuinely recreational. Hence the private order is far from being what it should be in representative democracies, and it certainly needs to be rejuvenated so that it can make a greater contribution to the moulding of the souls of men and women and children.

In representative democracies the *public order* has reached its highest development. Enormous corporations, whose organizations reach around and into all corners of the earth, have been especially characteristic of the leading free peoples. To a very large extent these corporations control the opportunities for the realization of ambition for millions of human beings. Many of them conduct their own training schools so that their employees may be thoroughly cognizant of all the details of the business and of its intricate organization. These industrial corporations are often closely interlocked with banks and investment houses, through which the financial aspects of the business are handled. In most cases the extent of this interlocking is kept as secret as possible. The result is that big business corporations have become so powerful and influential as to threaten the state's hegemony within the public order. Just as the play, sport, and "polite society" institutions of the private order threaten the dominant position of the family within that order, so do the powerful economic institutions threaten the dominant position of the political state within the public order. Perhaps this is the greatest threat to the perpetuation of the free institutions of representative democracies. Some fear that it may conceivably go on to the point where the free peoples of the earth will actually be ruled by an oligarchical régime of big business men. Indeed, certain critics hold that this is already the case, but we will postpone consideration of this criticism until after we have dicussed the status of the cultural order.

In representative democracies the *cultural order* is highly developed. The stimulus which the institutions of such governments give to individual initiative has caused a luxuriant growth of creative endeavor. This has greatly enriched human knowledge of nature as expressed in inventions and in the rapid expansion of the physical and biological sciences. It is within the great representative democracies that the best scientific laboratories, experimental research stations, scientific and other learned societies, natural history museums, libraries, and technical scientific journals on the face of the globe today are to be found. Nor is this stimulus to culture confined to science, as is sometimes implied by critics of representative democracy. For there is a tremendous interest in art in all of its forms. Indeed, many new art forms hitherto unknown have been created by the free peoples of the world. The Century of Progress Exhibition at Chicago has done a great deal of good in calling to the attention of the masses of the people the enormous advances that have been made in science and technology, and it has also given some attention to the fine arts. But, unfortunately, the achievements in literature and music are not so easily brought to the attention of the masses as are those in which the medium of expression is more tangible. Nevertheless the contributions to literature and to music by the gifted citizens of representative democracies during the last hundred years have probably enriched humanity more than similar contributions in any other century of human history. Only time can determine the full significance of these contributions, for their influence will extend into the centuries that are to come. But modern democracies have undoubtedly fostered in countless ways the production, enhancement, and conservation of the cultural values. They have not neglected the cultural order so far as science and arts are concerned.

How about their treatment of religion? Here the progress is certainly not so notable. Dominated by the absurd notion that religion should be isolated from the other aspects of the cultural order, representative democracies have permitted it to be shoved into the background. For the most part they have left the support of its institutions entirely to the voluntary efforts of the faithful. As a result innumerable sects and "isms" have arisen, and this progress has been allowed to go so far that it has undoubtedly weakened religion within the lands governed by representative democracies. To be sure, the religious institutions have profited in various ways by the progress that has occurred in other aspects of culture. But the chief weakness of the cultural order in representative democracies is to be found in the over-emphasis that has been placed on science and art as compared to religion. This is likely seriously to affect the qualities of character of the people, even to such an extent as to make future citizens of representative democracies incapable of maintaining their governments. For we must remember that this form of government reached its present powerful position in the world under the leadership of men who were reverent and God-fearing. The decay of religion in representative governments is too serious a matter to be neglected. Religion calls men to seek perfection. Reverence inculcates humility. But democracy loves mediocrity. She is inclined to stone those who offer counsels of perfection, and to cast out of her villages and cities those whose achievements rise too high above those of the majority.

REPRESENTATIVE DEMOCRACIES 143

In general we should give close heed to the wise and constructive criticism of our greatest living American philosopher. Referring to the shallowness of our culture and our failure to develop an adequate indigenous philosophy John Dewey says: "There is energy and activity among us, enough and to spare. Not an inconsiderable part of the vigor that once went into industrial accomplishment now finds its way into science; our scientific 'plant' is coming in its way to rival our industrial plants. Especially in psychology and the social sciences an amount of effort is putting forth which is hardly equalled in the rest of the world. He would be a shameless braggart who claimed that the result is as yet adequate to the activity. What is the matter? It lies, I think, with our lack of imagination in generating leading ideas. Because we are afraid of speculative ideas, we do, and do over and over again, an immense amount of dead, specialized work in the region of 'facts.' We forget that facts are only data; that is, are only fragmentary, uncompleted meanings, and unless they are rounded out into complete ideas—a work which can only be done by hypotheses, by a free imagination of intellectual possibilities—they are as helpless as are maimed things and as repellent as are needlessly thwarted events." [2]

[2] John Dewey in the *Proceedings of the Sixth International Congress of Philosophy*, pp. 541 f. Edited by E. S. Brightman and published by Longmans, Green and Company. Reprinted in D. S. Robinson's *An Anthology of Recent Philosophy*, pp. 51 f. Crowell)

4. An Examination of Two Criticisms of Representative Democracies

The Marxians hold that democracy is so deeply enmeshed in the evils of capitalism that it can never escape the inevitable disintegration of that economic system. They are evolutionists, and they argue that there is a goal of social evolution beyond democracy, namely, Marxian socialism with its classless society. They seek to weaken and to undermine all of the representative democracies by promulgating propaganda among the masses until the majority are persuaded that democracy is hopelessly antiquated as a form of government. When this propagandizing has been carried to this point the Marxians hope that representative democracies will be replaced by a soviet or some other socialistic form of government. Then all of the peoples of the earth will have destroyed their masters, and the dictatorship of the proletariat will everywhere dominate.

Two answers may be made to this criticism. In the first place there is no such necessary connection between capitalism and democracy as the socialists assume. We have pointed out that there is a danger that the economic institutions may come to control all of the institutions of representative democracies, but there is no such control at present. And there need never be. Business can be kept in its place, and we believe that the people will create and are creating ways of keeping it in its place. And secondly, we have proven conclusively that the soviet system of government is a lower form than democracy by our application of the postulates and three orders of an ideal state to both types. There is every reason to believe that the soviet system will develop into a new form of representative democracy. In fact, this eventuality is far more likely than that it will displace democracy. For there are many lands in which democracy has held sway for so long that their inhabitants would never tolerate a dictatorship of the proletariat.

The Fascists refer to the democratic form of government as "The Liberal State," and argue that it is an inherently weak form of government because it fosters the growth of all kinds of classes, which then seek to gain the ends of their own members to the point of injuring the government itself. Only a totalitarian state, one which absolutely dominates every class and institution under its jurisdiction, can overcome this weakness. The answer to this objection is that the free peoples of the world have learned how to develop an elaborate set of checks and balances, which absolutely prevent any one class of citizens from enslaving the rest of the population. In fact, the liberal state consists of these checks and balances, and being the creation of the people, it is continually subjected to their control. No bureaucrat and no alliance of bureaucrats can ever usurp the power of sovereignty in a true representative democracy, for it resides in the people; and a people that has learned self-government will never surrender that power. Abraham Lincoln was right when he said that you can fool all of the people part of the time, and some of the people all of the time, but you can never fool all of the people all of the time.

5. General Conclusion

In 1931 it was the author's privilege to spend the summer in France and Germany. While in Paris he took a trip through the battlefields of the World War, especially along the famous Hindenberg Line, and during the day visited the Forêt de Compiègne where the Armistice was signed. This is a most interesting place to visit, and especially for one who served as an officer in the United States Navy during the war. There is an open clearing in the forest and a building at one end of it houses the railroad car in which the Armistice was signed. This building was erected with funds contributed by Mr. Arthur Henry Fleming of Pasadena, California, in order that the famous car might be preserved as a permanent monument to the historic event which took place in it. A little forward and to the right of this building are the sites where this car and the car occupied by the German plenipotentiaries stood while the Armistice was being negotiated. Enclosing these sites the French government has erected an imposing plaza in the center of which is a large plaque, with the place occupied by the German car marked by posts and chains on one side of this plaque and that by the French car similarly marked

REPRESENTATIVE DEMOCRACIES

on the other side. Emblazoned on the plaque in letters of bronze are the words: *Ici le 11 Novembre 1918 succomba le criminel orgueil de L'Empire Allemand vaincu par les peuples libres qu'il pretendait asservir.* Translated into English this inscription reads: "Here the 11th of November 1918 succumbed the criminal pride of the German Empire, vanquished by the free peoples whom it tried to enslave." A cement walk leads to the opposite end of the clearing, where there is a rectangular stone monument with a window-like opening through the central shaft. In this opening there is a bronze sword pointed downward with the bronze image of a dead eagle lying at its point. This monument is the French sculptor's conception of the defeat of Germany.

I must confess that I did not like the sentence inscribed on the plaque. The wise proverb: "Pride goeth before a fall" at once occurred to me, suggested no doubt by the words "criminal pride." But there are different kinds of pride. There is the pride of the German leaders, who expected to win the World War but who were conquered. And that is the pride which the inscription calls criminal. We need not argue the question of whether it was criminal. For there is also the pride of those who conquered, a pride expressed by the inscription itself and by the down-pointed sword and the dead eagle. And this pride I did not like to see expressed in letters of bronze and with a down-pointed sword of bronze and the bronze image of a dead eagle.

To be sure, these are monuments to a mighty victory, which was won because some of the free peoples of the world united to withstand the attack of those who threatened to enslave them. They are truly symbolical of the united strength of these free peoples. What these peoples did in the World War they could doubtless do again. But why gloat over it? Why should the free peoples of the world act like a rooster who crows over his rival? Such cockiness breeds hatred in the conquered.

Shortly after visiting the place where the Armistice was signed, I went to the Rhineland, arriving only a few days after the French army of occupation finally evacuated this region. Old Heidelberg was just outside the area of occupation, and I spent three days there. Walking along the bank of the river Neckar I came face to face with a large paper sign that was painted on one of the official sign boards of the city. It was issued by the officials of the German youth movement, and it, too, contained a picture of the same-styled sword I saw pointed downward in the monument at the Forêt de Compiègne. But here it was a flaming red sword pointed upward, and across it were printed the ten commandments of the German youth, who was asked never to forget the wrong that was done to Germany by the Treaty of Versailles. And then I realized why I did not like the inscription on the plaque. It was symbolical of the kind of pride that breeds hate.

Remembering Woodrow Wilson's two famous

slogans when the United States entered the war: that this was a war to make the world safe for democracy, and a war to end war, I realized that the harsh terms of the Armistice and of the Treaty of Versailles had falsified those slogans and partially nullified the victory.

Let us recall the eternal moral truth which Shakespeare put into the mouth of Portia in the *Merchant of Venice:*

> The quality of mercy is not strain'd,
> It droppeth as the gentle rain from heaven
> Upon the place beneath: it is twice blest;
> It blesseth him that gives and him that takes:
> 'Tis mightiest in the mightiest: it becomes
> The throned monarch better than his crown;
> His sceptre shows the force of temporal power,
> The attribute to awe and majesty,
> Wherein doth sit the dread and fear of kings;
> But mercy is above this sceptred sway;
> It is enthroned in the heart of kings,
> It is an attribute to God himself;
> And earthly power doth then show likest God's
> When mercy seasons justice.

Mercy was not enthroned in the hearts of the democrats who made the Treaty of Versailles, and mercy did not season justice in that famous document. Thus in one of the most crucial moments of human history, representative democracies stand condemned because they placed temporal power above spiritual power, and thereby made the world unsafe for democracy and lost the war to end war.

The Allies, by their pride of victory and the injustice which that pride wrote into the peace treaty, produced a set of postwar conditions in Europe which may force them to fight another war to make the world safe for democracy, another war to end war. Should that war materialize and also end in a victory for the free peoples of the world, it is devoutly to be hoped that they may suppress their pride and make a peace expressive of their gratitude and humility. For only such a peace can sever the circle of retribution and forever end the hatred which breeds war. But let us fervently hope that such a peace can be achieved without another war, since the democratic form of government will be threatened until it is achieved.

Is this a vain hope? Is it really impossible for states and peoples to deal gently and mercifully with one another? We will discuss this question at some length in the next chapter. But all lovers of representative democracy may find some reassurance in a recent proclamation entitled *Liberty and Democracy,* which was prepared by a number of the leading citizens of Great Britain, and was widely published over their signatures. In this remarkable document the trend towards violence and dictatorships is strongly condemned, and a call is issued for a new leadership capable of reconstructing democracy. Here are the three brief concluding paragraphs:

"We, for our part, believe that power of action can be given to a democratic state whilst at the same time liberty is preserved to the individual citizen. If modern democracy is to survive, the electors must not be threatened or played down to; they must be informed, convinced, and led.

"We believe that at this moment we have in Britain a public that is anxious beyond all precedent for calm, efficient, and active leadership of this type. This public is ready to respond to the methods of reason by supporting a courageous, constructive, and democratic lead. By this way, and not by the way of violence, can an opportunity be offered for applying to our economic life the principles of order and design without the sacrifice of spontaneity and freedom.

"For this purpose we need a political method which combines (1) a profound conviction of the supreme importance of liberty, (2) an appreciation of the urgency of securing peace and justice by reorganization without delay in both international and national affairs, (3) a determination to work through democracy, as the primary safeguard of liberty, and (4) a conception of leadership that involves treating democracy with a new respect, offering scientific schemes of a far-sighted and far-reaching order, commending them by the methods of reason and asking that they be judged on their merits alone." [3]

It is to be hoped that some such proclamation may be adopted as a program of reform by all

[3] From the proclamation as published in the *Manchester Guardian*, Feb. 23, 1934. See also the *London Times*, Feb. 15, 1934.

lovers of representative democracy, regardless of the particular country of which they may happen to be citizens. If a World Parliament, made up of lay delegates from all the free peoples of the earth, could assemble at The Hague or in Geneva and draft such a proclamation, it might be possible to force upon the political leaders of the several representative democracies the kind of reorganization in both national and international affairs demanded in the concluding paragraphs of the British proclamation. A new and disastrous World War is in all probability the only other alternative, and nobody knows whether representative democracy as a form of government can survive another war.

What to Read

There is a good article by Brand Whitlock on *Democracy* in the 14th edition of the *Encyclopedia Britannica*. See also the article entitled *Government* in Hastings' *Encyclopedia of Religion and Ethics*. Francis W. Coker's *Recent Political Thought*, Pt. II "The Controversy over Democracy" gives an excellent survey of the arguments for and against democracy, with copious references at the end of each chapter. A good classical defense of democracy is John Stuart Mill's *Considerations on Representative Government*, and one of the most authoritative treatises is James Bryce's *Modern Democracies*, 2 vols. Alan F. Hattersley: *A Short History of Democracy*, and James H. Tufts: *America's Social Morality: Dilemmas of the Changing Mores* are important recent books. See also the article entitled "The Alleged Failure of Democracy" by R. B. Perry in the *Yale Review*, Vol. XXIV, pp. 37-51.

REPRESENTATIVE DEMOCRACIES

The critics of democracy are numerous. Some of the most important recent works are the following: Irving Babbitt: *Democracy and Leadership;* Ralph Adams Cram: *The Nemesis of Mediocrity;* Dorothy Crisp: *The Rebirth of Conservatism,* Ch. III; Christopher Hollis: *The American Heresy;* William R. Inge: *Labels and Libels;* Alleyne Ireland: *Democracy and the Human Equation;* Frank R. Kent: *Political Behavior;* A. M. Ludovici: *The False Assumptions of Democracy;* William MacDougall: *Is America Safe for Democracy?;* H. L. Mencken: *Notes on Democracy;* Robert Michels: *Political Parties: a Sociological Study of the Oligarchical Tendencies of Modern Democracy,* translated from the Italian by Eden and Cedar Paul; José Ortega y Gasset: *The Revolt of the Masses,* translated from the Spanish; Albert E. Wiggam: *The Fruit of the Family Tree* and *The New Decalogue of Science.*

The defenders of democracy are equally numerous. Some of the best recent books are: Ivor Brown: *The Meaning of Democracy;* Cecil D. Burns: *Democracy: Its Defects and Advantages;* S. Parkes Cadman: *Christianity and the State,* Lecture V; Edward P. Cheney: *Law in History and Other Essays,* Ch. IV; Edward S. Corwin: *The Democratic Dogma and the Future of Political Science and Other Essays,* 1st essay; W. E. Hocking: *Man and the State,* Chs. XXVIII-XXIX; A. D. Lindsay: *The Essentials of Democracy;* R. M. MacIver: *The Modern State,* pp. 351-420; Edward M. Sait: *Democracy;* T. V. Smith: *The American Philosophy of Equality* and *The Democratic Way of Life;* Roger Soltau: *French Political Thought in the Nineteenth Century,* Ch. XIII; Leonard Woolf: *After the Deluge: a Study of Communal Psychology;* Henry Wilkes Wright: *The Moral Standards of Democracy.*

John Dewey's *Democracy and Education*, and Charles W. Morris' *Pragmatism and the Crisis of Democracy* are valuable. See also F. J. C. Hearnshaw: *Social and Political Ideas of Some Representative Thinkers of the Victorian Age*, and Charles W. Morris' introduction to George H. Mead: *Mind, Self and Society*. See also John Dewey's article *A Critique of American Civilization* in the book edited by Kirby Page entitled *Recent Gains in American Civilization*, pp. 268-276.

CHAPTER VIII

THE APPLICATION OF ETHICAL PRINCIPLES TO INTERNATIONAL RELATIONS

1. Extent to Which Ethical Principles Are Applicable to International Relations

In preceding chapters our main interest has been in the application of ethical principles to the relations between a state and its own nationals, both as individual persons and as groups. In the rest of the book we will be dealing with the application of ethical principles to the relations between sovereign states and also to the relations between such states and backward peoples. Here we are beset with even worse difficulties than we had to meet before, and we may as well face one of these difficulties at once. It concerns the basic issue of whether relations between sovereign states, and between such states and culturally backward peoples, are within or without the jurisdiction of ethical judgment, and if they are within it, then to what extent.

Political realists take the position of Machiavelli: "When the entire safety of a country is at stake, no consideration of what is just or unjust, merciful or cruel, praiseworthy or shameful,—must intervene."

It has always been the basic assumption of most of the men of action who are actually in charge of governmental affairs that there are "reasons of state" that justify acts which would be highly reprehensible and even criminal in an individual. As Cavour put it: "If we did for ourselves what we do for our country, what rascals we should be." In the *Three Musketeers* Alexander Dumas makes effective use of this idea. According to Dumas, Cardinal Richelieu wrote a note which read: "It is by my order and for the good of the State that the bearer of this has done what he has done," so that Lady de Winter might escape punishment for the contemplated murder of D'Artagnan which she had planned. In one of the most dramatic scenes in the story Athos took the note away from her at the point of a pistol and gave it to D'Artagnan, who later used it to justify the executioner's act of killing Lady de Winter. Reasons of state—what crimes have been committed and then justified by this phrase!

It would be a gross error to think that this kind of political realism is no longer held or even to minimize its importance in contemporary thought. There are many able statesmen and political philosophers in active life today who are ardent defenders of this position. They advocate the principle that might makes right so far as international relations are concerned, and hold that states really have no duties other than those determined by the principle of their own self-preservation. This position

INTERNATIONAL RELATIONS

has recently been well expressed by Admiral Sims in an address made after his return from a disarmament conference, as reported in the *Boston Transcript:* "There was really no such thing as international good will. As everybody knows, 'war' exists at all times between all nations that trade with each other. It is an intensive struggle ... in which each nation strives for its own trade advantage without any particular consideration for its influence upon other nations. ... The ill-feeling that undoubtedly exists between nations on account of the economic war must be resolved before there can be any real hope of world peace. It is as if the world were a caldron of boiling oil around which the statesmen stand dropping in pieces of ice from time to time to keep the caldron from boiling over while at the same time new fuel is being heaped underneath the economic strife."[1]

Undoubtedly many contemporary world events support political realism. In recent years there has been a recrudescence of chauvinistic economic nationalism which many would have judged impossible a decade ago. In fact the various actual states of the earth are all now engaged in waging what is virtually an economic warfare, and in this conflict it seems impossible to secure general agreement on any rule of reason whatsoever. The nations have apparently gone insane in their efforts to

[1] Quoted by W. E. Hocking, *The Spirit of World Politics*, p. 495, from the Boston *Evening Transcript*, June 6, 1931. Reprinted by permission of The Macmillan Company, publishers.

preserve themselves from the consequences of the unprecedented economic depression, and such efforts as they are making only make international relations a confusion worse confounded. In such a time as this it is not surprising that the political realists are chuckling over the defeat of those whom they dub sentimentalists and fanatical idealists because of their advocacy of the doctrine that ethical principles are applicable to international relations.

At the other extreme from the political realists are the rigoristic moralists who hold that all ethical principles are just as applicable to international relations as they are to personal relations. Even so great a statesman as John Bright defended this extreme view in an address in which he said: "The House knows that for forty years I have endeavored to teach my countrymen an opinion and doctrine which I hold, namely, that the moral law is intended not only for individual life but for the life and practice of states in their dealings with one another. I think that in the present case there has been a manifest violation both of international law and of the moral law, and therefore it is impossible for me to give my support to it." [2] Undoubtedly there are many intelligent leaders today who are in full sympathy with the principle here enunciated by Bright.

Nevertheless, moral rigorism shares with political realism the defect of being an extreme view.

---

[2] Quoted by Charles H. Stockston in *Outlines of International Law*, p. 7, from Trevelyan's *Life of Bright*.

We may clarify the whole situation by comparing the relation between international political ethics and international law with the relation between personal ethics and municipal law. It has been rightly said that municipal law embodies *the ethical minimum* and depends upon ethics both historically and logically. This means that secular law has evolved out of a body of common sense morality and that only that portion of personal morals gets embodied in municipal law which can be enforced upon the majority of the citizens of a state. Now international political ethics is narrower in scope than personal morals within a single state. That is to say, there is a smaller portion of the total content of morality that is applicable to international relations than to the personal relations between human beings. And international law may be said to be the ethical minimum of international political ethics. So we may say that the relation between international political ethics and international law is analogous to the relation between ethics and municipal law. But this analogy does not carry with it an analogy between states and individuals, and it is, in fact, an indication that here there are perforce some essential differences.

Our position, then, is that ethical principles are applicable to the relations between states, but not to the same extent and in the same way as they are applicable to relations between persons. In the pregnant phrase of Professor Hocking, states are "ethically queer." Let us examine this queerness.

2. The Ethical Queerness of States

In his recently published monumental work entitled *The Spirit of World Politics* Professor Hocking discusses five basic differences between states and persons as ethical agents and taken together they constitute what he calls "the ethical queerness of states."

(1) *Uniqueness of each state.*—Generally speaking, individual human beings are very much alike in the sense that they form a natural species of organic nature and have a common biological structure. To be sure, there is a sense in which every person is unique and this fact must always be taken into account in ethical theorizing. Nevertheless, states are much more unique than are individuals. This extreme uniqueness of states is partly due to the geographical region over which each state has sovereignty. For example, a vast continental territory like Mexico is entirely different from the islands constituting the home land of the Japanese people. This geographical uniqueness carries with it other kinds of uniqueness. What a tropical or an island people need in the way of economic goods is quite different from what the people of a mountainous land or a cold climate need. There is a theory, invented by the German scientist Ratzel, that geographical considerations determine completely the character of a culture. We need not go as far as Ratzel and his followers in stressing the importance of climate and other geographical factors on the

development of culture, but we must recognize that each state is unique in an entirely different and much more extreme sense than each person is unique. And this leads to important differences in the application of ethical principles to states.

(2) *The puzzles of identity.*—Personal identity is often a puzzling problem in the case of individuals, as cases of mental aphasia and dual or multiple personality prove. But generally speaking, persons retain their identity and the continuity of their development much more than states. No one can deny conscious continuity to be the normal feature of personal growth and this makes it possible to hold individuals accountable for their acts, since the same individual who performs the act must also suffer its consequences. This is not true in the case of states. It is a fact that states often endure longer than even the oldest person. Hence the state is even more certain of reaping what it sows than is the person during the shorter span of his earthly life. Nevertheless, it is the whole person who acts and who is responsible for his act, whereas only a part of the state acts, namely, the governing part. When the party in power changes in a state the continuity is broken so that identity in a state is modified by every change of government, whereas each person remains essentially identical throughout his entire life. Often there is a wide gap between the government which makes a promise, and the one which has to fulfill that promise, and such a chasm rarely exists in the case of individuals who make

promises. The continuity of states, lacking consciousness, is less real than the conscious continuity of persons, so that ethical principles that are applicable to individuals may not be at all applicable to states, or may be applicable to them in a different way.

(3) *Property.*—In some ways property is more important to states than it is to individuals, since a state without any territory ceases to exist as a sovereign power, whereas many citizens of a state are virtually without private property. In this respect property is less under the control of states than it is under the individuals who use it, since these individuals really *own* and *use* the property over which the state merely *governs*. Only in a state in which all the land is owned by the government would the state's property become identical with that of the citizens, but as we have already learned, not even the Soviet State has been able entirely to destroy private ownership of the land. It follows that the idea of property is entirely different when applied to states and when applied to individual owners.

(4) *Existence.*—Self-preservation is supposed to be the first law of life. But self-preservation is quite different when applied to individuals and when applied to states. In one sense of the word a state's continuous existence is of far greater moment than that of any private citizen. For the destruction of the political state throws the whole of a culture into a chaotic wreck. Everything must be rebuilt from

the ground up. Yet a new state arises Phoenix-like from the wreckage of the old. So the existence of the state is really of less consequence than the existence of the individual. A state can die without a single member in it losing his life. Yet if it dies the life of every individual in it is so deeply affected that there are few who would not rather die than see their own state utterly destroyed. An individual's death hardly affects the state. These facts indicate the vast difference between existing and ceasing to exist, in the case of individuals and of states.

(5) *Vital Interests.*—To a state vital interests are important. Every state is always more deeply concerned with perpetuating its existence or with maintaining its security from aggression than any individual is ever concerned with keeping himself alive. Every problem that arises in international relations tends to be caught up into some vital interest, and to a state a vital interest is enough to justify and to place outside the realm of ethical consideration almost any action. Vital interests play a much less important rôle in the lives of civilized individuals. In a well ordered state nearly everybody takes the security of his own person for granted.

3. THE FIRST APPROACH TO THE APPLICATION OF ETHICAL PRINCIPLES TO INTERNATIONAL RELATIONS

With these basic differences before us let us now attempt to apply ethical principles to international relations. In making this attempt two different approaches are possible. We may consider current international relations that have become acute since the World War, and inquire whether the present actual states of the earth, functioning through their existing governments, are ethical in their dealings with each other today. More specifically, are the three greatest representative democracies—Great Britain, France, and the United States—ethical in their present-day relations to each other? Are the relations between these various states under their existing governments and Germany under Hitler ethical? Are their relations to the Soviet State under Stalin and to Italy under Mussolini ethical? Are their relations to the present Japanese government ethical? When we ask such questions we are faced with the unavoidable fact that we are too near to these contemporary international relations to judge how far they are ethical and how far they are unethical. But this does not mean that these relations are beyond the jurisdiction of ethics. Thinkers living one hundred years from now, who will be able to judge our contemporary international relations in the light of their effects throughout the century, will be able to determine to what extent these relations are ethical. But when we use this first approach all that we can do is to lay down certain general principles that seem inviolable, and use them to bring out the differences between international political ethics and personal ethics. And that we shall do presently.

However, before turning to this task, let us indicate briefly the other approach to the application of ethical principles to international relations. We may look back over the entire history of West European Culture, and inquire whether any important ethical ideas have been conceived, and then actualized in real institutions during that period of approximately two millennia. This second approach to our problem has recently been very effectively used by Professor A. N. Whitehead, and we shall expound it at some length in our next two sections. But now let us see how far the first approach will take us.

We accept two ethical principles of Professor Hocking. (1) *States are subjects of rights just as much as are individuals*. The proof of this is that states contain members who are moral beings capable of caring for each other. Even though states are themselves incapable of experiencing pleasure and pain, there are members of every state who are capable of recognizing that the independent political existence of other states than their own is desirable and necessary to the highest development of their own state. And this makes it possible for states to be subjects of rights just as much as individuals are. It becomes a matter of concern to every reflective mind that states should be conserved in order that cultural values may not perish from the earth. (2) *"The fundamental principle of right is the same for states as for individuals."* This moral principle is good will and the active endeavor to use one's power for the promotion of good everywhere. There is no reason why states should not be friendly towards one another, and just in their dealings with each other.

Now when we consider special applications of this principle of good will we discover the difference between international political ethics and personal ethics. For the essential differences pointed out above make it impossible to apply the principle of good will to states in the same way that we apply it to individuals. Some specific examples will make this clear and indicate exactly where the limitations fall. They prove that the scope of personal ethics is much wider than the scope of political ethics.

Take first the problem of distributive justice. This would demand that states should pay their debts instead of repudiating them, and keep their promises made in treaties instead of calling them scraps of paper. It would also demand that they treat large and small states alike. We may lay down the principle for personal ethics that we should be a person and treat others as persons, but we cannot lay down this principle for states. For states are not persons and the uniqueness of each state makes it impossible for any one state to treat all others alike. Each state needs something different from every other state. To be sure every state has its rights, but equality is at a minimum among states. They are actually extremely unequal. Hence debt-paying and treaty-breaking are not quite on the same level between states as between individuals. And from the fact that an individual should pay his debts one cannot infer that states should always pay theirs. Debt repudiation may be a necessity for a state even more than for an individual. Or those governing may think that it is and in practice the result is the same. Moreover, our bankruptcy laws permit individuals to repudiate their debts.

On the other hand, forbearance and patience are easier for a state to practice than for an individual. It is customary for states not to act against one another on the basis of a single dispute but only after a series of abuses. Giving way to wrath, impulsive action generally, is common among individuals. States usually act slowly.

Consider next forgiveness and non-resistance. These virtues are possible for individuals and they are truly ethical when they are so practiced as to make the person toward whom they are directed change his ways. For when they are so practiced they generate in others the attitude of forgiveness and of non-resistance. States cannot practice good will in this extreme form. Every state must resist invasions from hostile states. No state can forgive another state for acts that are definitely injurious. But states can and often do forgive in the sense that they resume friendly relations with other states after breaking relations with them. Debt cancellation is sometimes practiced and this is an economic policy that simulates forgiveness.

Our conclusion is that the ethical principle of good will is applicable to the dealings of states with one another, and that some personal attitudes can be transferred to international relations whereas other personal attitudes cannot be. But we refrain from passing judgment on contemporary international relations on the ground that contemporaries are incapable of determining what specific actions of states are ethical and what are unethical. Statesmen who have to initiate such actions must rely on their own intuitions and on divine guidance, but they may rest assured that what they initiate will be judged by posterity and that their own place in history will be determined by that judgment and not by the plaudits or the curses which they happen to receive from their contemporaries.

4. The Second Approach to the Application of Ethical Principles to International Relations

In all probability those who dwell continually upon the mess that the world is now in are unable to think clearly, just because of the din and the uproar that has been raised by the World War and its aftermath of large scale readjustment. The spirit of the times, what the Germans call *Zeitgeist*, of this postwar era distracts and overwhelms thinkers, more perhaps than any other *Zeitgeist* has ever done. The best way to comprehend the real meaning of current world events is to look at them from the perspective of the entire course of West European history. Professor Whitehead has rendered a significant service to those thinkers who continue to hold an optimistic view of western culture by giving the interpretation of its development which he has worked out in his *Adventures of Ideas*. He has proven conclusively that economic and political issues really are less important in the final evaluation of what states are doing than are the moral ideals which are being actualized by the actions of states. Let us examine in some detail his theory of the way in which political actions are subservient to those moral principles and ideals which are realized through them.

Professor Whitehead thinks that history is the story of the way in which some very general ethical ideas are grasped, and are then gradually applied to various aspects of the social order until they completely transform it. Naturally this is a slow process, and its slowness is not wholly due to human inefficiency. It is largely due to the fact that no way can be found to make the modification which the idea demands without either destroying the social order or introducing worse evils than the one the idea is seeking to correct. "Successful progress," Professor Whitehead says, "creeps from point to point, testing each step." . . . "A great idea in the background of dim consciousness is like a phantom ocean beating upon the shores of human life in successive waves of specialization." These sentences from Professor Whitehead's book suggest his method of interpreting history. And here is an illuminating passage in which he indicates the stages in this gradual application of general ethical ideas to transform the social order. These great ideas "start as speculative suggestions in the mind of a small, gifted group. They acquire a limited application to human life at the hands of various sets of leaders with special functions in the social structure. A whole literature arises which explains how inspiring is the general idea and how slight need be its effects in disturbing a comfortable society. Some transition has been produced by the agency of the new idea. But on the whole the social system has been inoculated against the full infection of the new principle. It takes its place among interesting notions which have a restricted application. But a general idea is always a danger to the existing order. The whole body of its conceivable special embodiments in various usages of society constitute a program of reform. At any moment the smouldering unhappiness of mankind may seize on such a program and initiate a period of rapid change guided by the light of its doctrines."[3] In this succinct statement Professor Whitehead summarizes the steps in which general ideas work themselves out in history, reconstituting the social order as they effectively penetrate its various institutions.

An excellent illustration of this process is the gradual victory of the ethical idea of freedom over the institution of human slavery, a process that has extended from about 400 B. C. down to our own time. Plato grasped the general idea of freedom when he conceived of the human soul as rational and as capable of contemplating the eternal ideas.

[3] From A. N. Whitehead: *Adventures of Ideas*, p. 17, by permission of The Macmillan Company, Publishers.

INTERNATIONAL RELATIONS 171

For this meant that man was not born to be the slave of some other man, but that each individual possesses a dignity and worth that is intrinsic. Yet Plato agreed with Pericles and Alexander the Great; and Cicero, Sulla, and Caesar agreed with these, their illustrious predecessors, in thinking that human slavery was absolutely essential to the maintenance of a social order in which some men could be free. Throughout the Hellenic and Hellenistic epochs of civilization it was believed by the best thinkers that a barbarous foundation was essential to the civilized superstructure of society. But today the best minds hold exactly the opposite political theory. "Slavery was the presupposition of political theorists then; freedom is the presupposition of political theorists now." (p. 15) The ancients found it hard to reconcile slavery with their humanitarian feelings, just as we find it hard to reconcile freedom with certain brute forces in modern life. Nevertheless ancients and moderns hold opposite views on the question of slavery versus freedom.

What has produced this reversal of political theory? It has been due to the gradual working out of Plato's conception of the intrinsic value of the human soul. It is not easy to trace all of the stages in this process from the running summary account which Professor Whitehead interweaves with other material. But here are some of the more important developments in the continuous process. First we find Plato and his more humane contemporaries revealing in their writings "an uneasy feeling about the compulsory degradation of mankind." We know, too, that there were kind-hearted slave holders in the ancient world, and that the Stoic lawyers of the Roman Empire formed the law to favor the slaves, using the principle that there are rights inherent in human nature. Thus slave rights came to be recognized. And yet none of the reformers of the ancient world directly attacked slavery as an institution. For over six hundred years the general idea of the moral worth of the individual leavened the institutions of the ancient world, but always under the definite restriction that slavery was regarded as necessary. According to Professor Whitehead a direct frontal attack on slavery as an institution at that time would have destroyed civilization. When Christianity came, it rapidly assimilated the Platonic doctrine of the intrinsic worth of the human soul. Yet it applied the idea to religion only and dreamed of another world to replace the actually existing social order. Hence its ethics was an *ad interim* ethics. And thus Christianity did not at the beginning, nor in the Middle Ages, nor during the Reformation make a direct frontal attack on slavery. At first it augmented the power of the moral idea of freedom, as we see, for example, in St. Paul's epistle to Philemon, but it soon became encrusted with the cake of custom.

The next great wave of triumph for the idea of freedom came with the sceptical humanitarianism

INTERNATIONAL RELATIONS 173

of the 18th century in France, which Professor Whitehead says "has remade the presuppositions of the civilized world, in speculation, in science, and in sociological premises." While this movement drew much of its inspiration from John Locke and other Englishmen of the 17th century, nevertheless the French thinkers clarified, broadened and universalized it. Out of this movement democracy was born and it finally freed the slaves. For democracy faced the institution of slavery directly and thoroughly. In its fight against slavery democracy was greatly aided by the Wesleyan religious revival and by the humanitarian ideal of Jeremy Bentham and Auguste Comte. Professor Whitehead concludes his account of the victory of freedom over slavery with this sentence: "Finally, the humanitarian movement of the 19th century, combined with a religious sense of the kinship of men, has issued in the settled policy of the great civilized governments to extirpate slavery from the world." (p. 35). Between the lines, to be sure, one can detect that Professor Whitehead is aware that even yet slavery exists in the form of forced labor in the colonies of some of the most highly civilized nations of the modern world. Nevertheless, he is right—the ultimate victory over human slavery is not far away when the institution is outlawed by common consent of mankind.

There is little hope that great sovereign states, whose citizens are wholly or partly enslaved, will ever be able to deal ethically with each other or with other sovereign states whose citizens are essentially free. We may adapt the immortal words of Abraham Lincoln to characterize the present international situation: *The world cannot remain half slave and half free.* One system will ultimately have to give way before the superior power of the other. We are faced with the disjunction: Either all of the major powers of the earth must become nations of free peoples, or the hope of an ethical international world order must be abandoned. Hence a further actualization of the idea of freedom is an indispensable preliminary to the development of an international political ethics.

5. THE GRADUAL ACTUALIZATION OF THE IDEA OF THE UNITY OF MANKIND

Unfortunately, Professor Whitehead has made no attempt to apply his method of tracing the gradual actualization of ethical ideas to one of the sublimest thoughts ever conceived by the mind of man: *the idea of an integral union of all mankind within which all will be treated as free persons.* However, two valuable pieces of recent research into the origin of this idea make it possible for us to suggest what such an application would be.[4]

Plato and Aristotle did not clearly grasp the idea of the unity of all mankind. As we have already

[4] See W. W. Tarn: *Alexander the Great and the Unity of Mankind* (Oxford University Press, 1933), and *The Political Philosophy of Hellenistic Kingship,* by Erwin R. Goodenough, published in *Yale Classical Studies,* Vol. I, pp. 55 ff. (Yale University Press, 1928).

INTERNATIONAL RELATIONS

indicated, both of these philosophers made a sharp distinction between Greeks and barbarians. Aristotle told his distinguished pupil, Alexander, to treat Greeks as free men and friends, but barbarians as slaves and animals. Plato taught in the *Republic,* and Aristotle agreed with him in his *Politics,* that all barbarians were enemies by nature, and that it is right to enslave and even to destroy them. To be sure, in the famous passage which is quoted below (see p. 263), Plato does seem to have grasped the idea of the unity of mankind negatively, since he suggests in it that the human race will never escape from its ills and woes until philosophers are kings, and this idea undoubtedly influenced the Hellenistic philosophy of kingship. Then, too, the cynic philosopher, Diogenes, called himself a cosmopolite, that is "a citizen of the universe," but in so doing he merely meant to emphasize the negative fact of his not being a citizen of any Greek city state.

Dr. Tarn argues persuasively that the real originator of the revolutionary idea of the unity of mankind was Alexander himself. He thinks that Alexander's prayer at a banquet celebrating a reconciliation among his followers, in which he prayed that his Macedonian and Persian soldiers might treat one another as brothers and partners in rule, is the first actual expression of this idea. He supports this thesis with much evidence. There is a famous passage in Plutarch which says that Alexander's intention was "to bring about, as between mankind generally, Homonoia and peace and fellowship and make them all one people" on the ground that "God is the common father of all men." The Greek word *Homonoia,* and the Latin word *Concordia* both mean "a union of hearts," a "being of one mind together," Unity and Concord among men.

The idea of the unity of mankind was taken over by Stoic philosophers in their doctrine of a world-state in which the essential unity of mankind was central, but with the important difference that they thought of this world-state as being already actual, and as requiring no effort on the part of any ruler to embody it in any existing government. The idea of the unity of mankind received a more detailed elaboration in the famous chain of progress found in a fragment of the philosopher Theophrastus, whose ideas were later popularized by Cicero. Theophrastus succeeded Aristotle, his teacher, as the head of the Peripatetic School, the Lyceum. He taught that all men are kin and he traced the growth of human love "from affection for one's family, to affection for one's fellow citizens, thence to affection for one's own race, and thence to affection for all men," and Dr. Tarn adds that "love might be a better translation." [5]

From that time onward, as Dr. Goodenough's research also proves, the Hellenistic philosophy of kingship revolved around the idea that a ruler's

[5] *Loco citato,* p. 20. Compare this chain of progress with the levels of social consciousness given in the table above, p. 29.

INTERNATIONAL RELATIONS

divine mission was to reconcile the enmities of men and to bring all races together in one common accord. It was every ruler's supreme duty to extend the bounds of the civilized world as far as possible by his conquests, and then to rule so beneficently and justly that all peoples under his sovereignty would be unified as brothers by the bond of Roman citizenship. We may consider the Roman Empire under Augustus as the highest culmination of this first actualization of the idea of the unity of mankind. Tiberius vowed as a private citizen to build a temple to the Imperial Concord achieved under the Emperor Augustus, and when he himself was Emperor he dedicated the famous temple *Concordia Augusta,* which it took him seventeen years to build. Figures of Mercury and Hercules flanked the main entrance to this magnificent temple. Here is Dr. Tarn's explanation of why these two figures were used for this purpose: "Mercury certainly stood for trade. Under the Empire the Greek cities of Asia struck innumerable coins to emphasize the Homonoia between themselves and other cities, and it has been shown that this refers to trade relations; it was widely believed that inter-city trade promoted unity and good will. But I have not myself seen Hercules explained. He can hardly be anything but the Heracles of Hellenistic philosophy, the ideal ruler and benefactor of mankind—no longer of Greeks alone, as before Alexander, but of all men. The temple of the Imperial Concord was to enshrine the spirit of a new age, an age of good will and unity." [6]

With the fall of the Roman Empire the Church attempted to bring about a second actualization of the idea of the unity of mankind. The conception of a Holy Roman Empire, composed of all of the Christian kings of the earth, with one of their number as temporal Emperor, but with all under the direct spiritual guidance of the Pope, replaced the older notion. But great schisms within the Church and the growth of strong modern nations made this actualization even less effective than the Imperial Concordia of Augustus.

As will be pointed out in the next chapter, modern philosophers have done a great deal to enrich the content of the idea of a unity of all mankind. And during the last two centuries other attempts have been made by great statesmen to actualize this idea. Castlereagh's "Conference of Ambassadors," which functioned for over six years, and which produced the European Concert, was probably the most important of these attempts during the nineteenth century. But the movement may be said to have culminated in the creation of the League of Nations, which will be discussed in some detail later.

Modern men's efforts to achieve a fuller actualization of the idea of freedom are fused with their efforts to achieve a fuller actualization of the idea of the unity of mankind. Our age is a transition period in which there is much weeping and gnash-

[6] *Loco citato*, p. 13.

ing of teeth. Numerous are the prophets of gloom who darken counsel for the myriads of suffering Jobs today. Nevertheless, despite all temporary upheavals, we have shown that the real Golden Age of humanity lies, not in the past, but beyond these tumultuous days in that period when a final synthesis of the actualizations of freedom and of the unity of mankind shall have been attained. Whether any of those who are now living ever enjoy that new age or not, they can help to create it by passing the torch of social progress to on-coming human beings. They or their children shall see such an era of Homonoia and Concordia, of peace and good will among the nations, as previous generations have never known. Although it is only too obvious that the kingdoms of this world have not yet become the Kingdom of God, we rejoice personally in having thought our way through the mists and fogs of confusion and obscurity which today envelop the good ship of state to a glimpse of the sunshine of a genuinely optimistic philosophy of history. Our next task is the clarification of this point of view with a discussion of the deeper meaning of civilization and of culture.

What to Read

In the second and third sections of this chapter we have followed closely W. E. Hocking's *The Spirit of World Politics,* Chs. XXVII and XXVIII, a book which is of the utmost importance to every student of the ethical aspects of international relations. In the fourth section we have utilized the deeply significant philosophy of history sketched by A. N. Whitehead's *Adventures of Ideas* (see especially Part I). Note also the references given in the footnote to section five. There is an informative article entitled *International Law, Public* in the 14th edition of the *Encyclopedia Britannica*. Consult also R. L. Buell: *International Relations* and A. S. Hershey: *The Essentials of International Public Law*. The first modern author to use the word *international* was Jeremy Bentham. See his *Principles of Morals and Legislation*, p. 326 (note).

In addition to Niccolo Machiavelli's *The Prince*, see Heinrich von Treitschke: *Politics*, 2 vols. (translated by Blanche Dugdale and Torben de Bille), for a classic defense of political realism. See also F. W. Coker: *Recent Political Thought*, Ch. XVI and the references there given. Among the criticisms of political realism the following are especially valuable: H. W. C. Davis: *The Political Thought of Heinrich von Treitschke;* Francis Delaisi: *Political Myths and Economic Realities*, Ch. IV; Carlton J. H. Hayes: *Essays on Nationalism;* W. E. Hocking: *Man and the State*, Ch. V; J. A. Leighton: *The Individual and the Social Order*, Ch. XLVI; Thomas G. Masaryk: *The Spirit of Russia*, 2 vols., translated by Eden and Cedar Paul (especially Chs. XV-XVI of Vol. II); Reinhold Niebuhr: *Moral Man and Immoral Society;* M. C. Otto: *Things and Ideals*, Ch. I; Pitirim Sorokin: *Contemporary Sociological Theories*, Ch. VI; John Watson: *The State in Peace and War;* and W. W. Willoughby: *Prussian Political Philosophy*.

Valuable books defending the application of ethics to international relations are: Bernard Bosanquet: *Social and International Ideals;* Herbert A. L. Fisher: *The Common Weal;* J. S. Mackenzie: *Fundamental Problems of Life;*

and Albert Schweitzer: *The Decay and the Restoration of Civilization,* translated by C. T. Campion.

See also Hans Driesch: *Ethical Principles,* and William MacDougall: *Ethics and Some Modern World Problems* (note especially the Appendix). See H. D. Lasswell's critique of the idea of the unity of mankind entitled "The Problem of World-Unity: in Quest of a Myth" in the *International Journal of Ethics,* Vol. XLIV, pp. 68-93, and the article entitled "Cosmopolitanism" in the *Encyclopedia of the Social Sciences.*

CHAPTER IX

CULTURAL MONISM VERSUS CULTURAL PLURALISM

1. Explanation of Terminology

In the last chapter we learned that Professor Whitehead appeals to the history of West European culture to prove that there has been a gradual actualization of ethical ideas in the struggles of the nations and peoples of this region of the earth over a period of more than two millennia. This shows that the full ethical implications of political functioning cannot be understood when we restrict attention to the contemporary jockeyings of states for economic advantage. We are forced to appeal to something beyond particular states and their transient governments to justify our thesis that ethical principles are applicable to the relations between states. What is that something beyond existing states and the actual governing power within these states? The answer is: culture as a whole and civilization. Are these then identical? And what are they? These are the questions we shall attempt to answer in this chapter.

Culture and civilization are not identical. There are many different senses in which each word is used. Some writers take civilization to be the wider term and others so define culture as to make it include civilization. Oswald Spengler, whose theory will be discussed at some length presently, even goes so far as to identify culture with the vital and creative part of the evolution of a people, and civilization with the period of decline and decay which follows when a people lose their virility. We can not follow Spengler in this complete shift in the meaning of the term civilization from something highly esteemed to something unworthy and decadent. Yet we must agree with him and with others who treat civilization as being only a part of culture.

Anthropologists contrast culture with racial factors. They define culture as that part of what a contemporary people inherit from their progenitors in the form of traditions which have to be learned, whereas the race-factor is an unlearned type of inheritance. They speak of three aspects of culture—language, material culture (arts and crafts), and moral culture (social institutions). Following the anthropologists we would include in a culture all of the higher creations of a people—their language, their literature, their painting, sculpture and architecture, their music, their religion, their science—in fact the sum total of their creative achievements as a community of living beings, from the beginning of their existence to the end, if end there be. A culture is the entire unified spiritual life of a people in their gradual advance from barbarism or savagery to the highest level of their creative achievements. But a culture also includes the movement downward from this apex even to the uttermost influence of the cultural achievements of that people after they cease to exist as an actual community. Thus we are using the term culture socially and not individually, and we are deliberately giving it as wide an extension as possible.

Civilization, as Spengler rightly recognizes, is a much more restricted term than culture, but it is the creative edge of a culture and not the stage of its decay. At least that is the sense in which we propose to use the term and it is undoubtedly the sense which is nearest to the ordinary usage. Let us think, then, of civilization as being that part of the evolution of a culture extending from the time when a people have mastered nature and organized their communal life sufficiently to emerge out of the mere gathering and hunting stage of their development until they finally lose their grip and become the slaves of some more virile people, if ever they do. And some certainly do. Archaeology proves that civilizations have waxed and waned in human history. And when they wane and finally entirely disappear, what becomes of their culture? Every civilization emerges out of a culture and, when it disappears, the culture out of which it emerged is transmitted to those who destroyed it. This has been the movement of human history.

Think for example of the ancient Egyptians. We see them emerge out of pre-history in the Nile Valley. They had a language, a religion, some art of a crude form, and certain technical skill. Unquestionably this much cultural content existed before there was an ancient Egyptian civilization. Enriched by the long period of creative striving of these people during their civilized existence, this culture was transmitted to others and ultimately to us. Ancient Egyptian civilization is dead but the culture of the ancient Egyptians lives on. Egyptologists know their language, museums preserve many of the objects of their material culture, and modern historians know what their religion and other social institutions were.

Is it not reasonable to assume that there is always a growing edge to culture, and that the rise and fall of civilizations is merely the rise and fall of particular states? May we not conceive of a creative principle which makes for the unity of all mankind, some mysterious urge that continually drives human beings forward to higher endeavor and richer achievement? The affirmative answer implied in these questions assumes that *human culture is really one* and that mankind has as a final goal the creation of a single highly advanced civilization. Let us call this view *cultural monism*. As a recent popular writer expresses it: "All history is one piece. It is a serial story, always 'to be continued in our next,' and the events of a hundred years ahead are in process of formation now. . . . The evolution of humanity is a slow movement from evil to good and from wrong to right."[1] According to this theory separate states and governments are but the transient instruments of the onward sweep of a human progress to which there will be no end. Obviously cultural monism is a highly optimistic philosophy of human history.

Or does every culture that emerges out of barbarism contain the germs of its own ultimate decay? Do cultures, like other living organisms, have a life-span extending from birth to death? The affirmative answer implied in these questions assumes that *there are many distinct human cultures*, each of which contains within itself a definite limited set of possibilities, having realized which it will die. Let us call this view *cultural pluralism*. On this view every people spends its creative energies in the realization of its latent possibilities, struggles with other peoples and finally succumbs before a more virile and youthful people, just as an old boxer yields the championship to a young challenger when age debilitates his skill. Spengler's form of this theory is a highly pessimistic philosophy of human history. Let us examine each of these theories.[2]

---

[1] T. Sharper Knowlson in *Think for Yourself*, p. 151, T. Werner Laurie, Ltd., Publishers, London.

[2] The terms here used to designate these opposite philosophies of history have been formed on the analogy of the terms *political monism* and *political pluralism*. Political monism is the theory that a people is a unified whole in which sovereignty resides, whereas political pluralism holds that sovereignty is split up and resides in numerous blocs and groups, which in their totality constitute the "invisible government." I first used the terms cultural monism and cultural pluralism in the sense explained above in my *Introduction to Living Philosophy* (Thomas Y. Crowell Co., 1932), pp. 338-341.

2. CULTURAL MONISM

There is a natural bias of the human mind towards cultural monism. Just as a child is unable to imagine itself not existing so the adult finds it exceedingly difficult to conceive of the cessation of the existence of the people whose traditions and glories, whose hopes and aspirations he shares. But this is not the whole of man's natural bias towards cultural monism. Every generation naturally thinks of itself as forming the crest of the great wave of cultural evolution. Previous generations, even back to the very beginning of *homo sapiens* on the earth, are treated as forerunners of contemporary civilization. Thus there is a monistic tendency in our naïve common sense way of viewing history. Every people tends to regard itself as the chosen people for which all history and all pre-history has been merely preparatory. After enumerating the great achievements of various Hebrew leaders the author of the *Epistle to the Hebrews* writes: "And these all, having had witness borne to them through their faith, received not the promise, God having provided some better thing concerning us, that apart from us they should not be made perfect." (*Hebrews* XI, 39 f., American Revised Version.) These verses epitomize the monistic philosophy implicit in the Christian interpretation of history, which is rooted back in the Jewish philosophy of the chosen people as expressed in the Messianic hope. Men naturally and almost inevitably regard the preservation and enhancement of their own culture as the goal of all human evolution. In this sense cultural monism may be regarded as the common sense philosophy of the human race.

A contemporary expression of this theory of cultural monism is the Nordic Myth, now being exploited by the German Nazis to prove that all human culture originated in the region now known as Germany. In *Mein Kampf* Herr Hitler wrote: "If we divide the human race into three categories —founders, maintainers, and destroyers of culture —the Aryan stock alone can be considered as representing the first category." In May, 1933, the Nazi Minister for the Interior, Dr. Frick, issued a circular to the educators of Germany in which he said: "The history of Europe is the work of people of Nordic race. . . . A decisive influence on the history of Hither Asia was exercised first by the Indians, Medes, Persians, and Hittites, originally of Nordic stock . . . who were eventually overwhelmed by the forces of foreign blood after they had created high civilizations in Persia and India." And in a speech at Nuremberg, the Nazi Commissar for Justice, Dr. Frank, said: "The blood substance of the Germanic race constitutes so preëminent and unique an asset of the world as a whole that we should be justified in counting it the duty of the entire human race to safeguard this basic Germanic element; for we know that from this racial substance have issued the highest achievements of man." [2]

[2] These quotations are from an article entitled "Anthropology and Herr Hitler," by V. Gordon Childe, published in the March 1934 number of *Discovery*, Vol. XV, p. 65.

MONISM VERSUS PLURALISM

The Nazis obtain a cultural monism by adapting and misinterpreting the antiquated racial theory of culture. For the old idea of physical race has been discredited by modern anthropology. It is now recognized that the notion of an Aryan race, as well as the identification of race with culture, is an absolutely false idea. One cannot prove cultural monism by tracing all of culture to a hypothetical race of Aryans or Nordics. Modern anthropological research demonstrates conclusively that there is no such thing as a pure race of mankind, and that the Nordic theory is a scientific fiction.

A more creditable form of cultural monism is to be found in the Hegelian philosophy of history. Hegel attempted to trace the evolution of states and forms of government from the oriental despotisms to modern constitutional monarchies. He assumed that this was a linear evolution in the direction of the realization of greater freedom for the individual. He laid down the basic principle: "It is only an inference from the history of the World, that its development has been a rational process; that the history in question has constituted the rational necessary course of the World-Spirit." And later on he says: "The history of the world is none other than the progress of the consciousness of Freedom; a progress whose development according to the necessity of its nature, it is our business to investigate. The general statement given above, of the various grades in the consciousness of Freedom—and which we applied in the first instance to

190 POLITICAL ETHICS

the fact that the Eastern nations knew only that *one* is free; the Greek and Roman world only that *some* are free; while *we* know that *all* men absolutely (man as *man*) are free—supplies us with the natural division of Universal History, and suggests the mode of its discussion." [3] Here is a cultural monistic philosophy, according to which human history is the unfolding of the Absolute Spirit. How utterly different is Hegel's cultural monism from that of the present Nazi régime in Germany!

The positive philosophy of Auguste Comte (positivism), especially as it is expressed in the now famous law of the three stages, is another important historical form of cultural monism. According to Comte man has evolved from a theological stage in which he interpreted every event by referring it to some god, through a metaphysical stage in which he interpreted events by bringing them under some abstract concept, to the scientific stage in which he discovered the scientific law explaining the event in question. This positivism of Comte and the Hegelian form of cultural monism have been merged by the Marxians in the development of their materialistic economic interpretation of history. On this view all of human history must be considered as the struggle of men to master the forces of nature—a struggle in which the hard working masses

[3] See J. Sibree's translation of Hegel's *Philosophy of History*, pp. 10 and 17. Note the similarity between Hegel's idea, and Whitehead's conception of a gradual actualization of ethical ideas in West European culture, especially as applied to the idea of freedom. (See above, pp. 168 ff.)

or proletariat have been cheated of the spoils of victory by shrewd capitalists.

Thus there are many different forms of cultural monism that are functioning in the world today. Advocates of the racial theory attempt to prove cultural monism by showing that one race of human beings is the source of all human culture. In the light of the facts such a theory is absurd. Only those forms of cultural monism which are philosophical are at all tenable. But they wrest the facts out of their natural context and force them to fit a preconceived theory. This is as true of the Hegelian forms of cultural monism as it is of the Comtean and Marxian forms. All of these philosophical forms of the theory are purely speculative. So far as the facts themselves are concerned, we must accept the judgment of Professor Marett: "Whatever the future may have in store, man has not hitherto faced his environment as a single community, united alike racially and culturally so far as interbreeding and mutual understanding can bring it about." [4] In other words, cultural monism is a hope for the future, it is not now and probably never has been an actual fact. The final actualization of the idea of the unity of mankind is yet to be achieved. If it ever was an actual fact, it was in that remote period of prehistory when mankind was in the so-called cradle of the race. And how do we know that there was just one cradle? The hypothesis

[4] See R. R. Marett's article entitled *Anthropology* in the 14th edition of the *Encyclopedia Britannica*, Vol. II, pp. 41 ff.

that there were many seems equally plausible and equally futile. For the facts at the beginning of prehistory are facts we can never know. But let us postpone our final evaluation of cultural monism, and turn to a more detailed consideration of cultural pluralism.

3. CULTURAL PLURALISM

The supreme apostle of gloom of our generation is Oswald Spengler. In two massive tomes entitled *Der Untergang des Abendslandes,* which Mr. C. F. Atkinson has translated into English under the title *The Decline of the West,* he delivers a slashing attack on cultural monism. We can best briefly summarize this attack by explaining what Spengler means by two epithets which he hurls at the monistic interpretation of history. He calls it the *tapeworm theory of history.* By this he means that the monists treat all other cultures as the suckers and segments of their own, just as the main body of a tapeworm is fed by the various tentacles which radiate from it. He also calls cultural monism *the Ptolemaic theory of history.* He writes: "The most appropriate designation for this current West European scheme of history, in which the great Cultures are made to follow orbits round us as the presumed centre of all world-happenings, is the Ptolemaic system of history. The system that is put forward in this work in place of it I regard as the Copernican discovery in the historical sphere, in that it admits no sort of privileged position to the

Classical or the Western Culture as against the cultures of India, Babylon, China, Egypt, the Arabs, Mexico—separate worlds of dynamic being which in point of mass count for just as much in the general picture of history as the Classical, while frequently surpassing it in point of spiritual greatness and soaring power." [5]

Spengler's own theory of cultural pluralism is suggested in the last sentence of the quotation. He works it out in great detail, applying it to every aspect of culture, for example, to architecture, music, literature, mathematics, et cetera. A summary of his interesting interpretation of culture can be given by explaining his idea of *a comparative morphology of world history* and his *analogy of the seasons*.

By the comparative morphology of world history Spengler means that the various stages in the evolution of one culture should be compared and contrasted with those in the evolution of another, and that the basic principle of a culture should be exhibited and contrasted with that of another. Thus the basic principle of West European culture he designates as the Faustian principle, and the basic principle of the Persian culture he calls the Magian principle. He chooses some unique feature of a culture and makes that its basic principle, using it to bring out the sharp contrast between it and dif-

[5] Oswald Spengler: *The Decline of the West*, Vol. I, p. 18. Translated by C. F. Atkinson (Knopf). See also his *The Hour of Decision* by the same translator and publisher, in which he deals with "Germany and world-historical evolution."

ferent cultures. His idea is that every culture contains a set of possibilities which are gradually actualized as it lives out the complete span of its existence. It follows that every culture goes through certain well-marked stages in its evolution, and that a comparison can be made between any of these stages in a given culture and the corresponding stage in some entirely different culture. This he calls the comparative morphology of world history —a science which he claims to have created.

The analogy of the seasons clarifies this conception. Spengler refers to the dawn of a culture out of barbarism, or out of the disintegration of an old civilization when it is destroyed by a wave of virility that sweeps over it from some less civilized region of the earth, as the Springtime of that culture. And the period when the art, literature, religion, and other aspects of a culture are growing and expanding he calls the Summertime. Later when men begin to reap the fruits of the creative work of their forefathers by building great cities and systems of transportation and communication they reach the Autumn of their culture. And this is the beginning of the end. For the cities grow at the expense of the provinces and all the energies of the people are absorbed in luxurious living. Creative art dies out and art museums take its place. Religion disintegrates. Civilization replaces culture. This is the Wintertime of the entire cultural process. After a people enter this stage there is no hope for them. Ere long they will become

MONISM VERSUS PLURALISM

dominated by some less civilized but more virile people, and their culture will disintegrate. Out of its ruins the process will start over again. The West European culture, which includes all the nations of Western Europe and of North and South America, together with the colonies of the French, Dutch, and English is in this last irremediable condition. Spengler gives it three or four more centuries in which to peter out. That is why we have called him the supreme apostle of gloom of our generation.

Spengler's theory of cultural pluralism has produced a voluminous literature. The cultural monists have attacked him furiously. They have even psychoanalyzed him and dismissed his theory as the natural product of a defeated but vain-glorious German. Unfortunately for this interpretation he developed the theory before the World War and when Germany was at the height of her power.

Spengler unquestionably overlooks one important fact about the evolution of a culture, and that is the rather frequent occurrence of a rejuvenation of a culture by some great cataclysm. This idea has been well developed by the Frenchman E. F. Gautier in articles entitled *L'Interpretation Biologique des Grandes Catastrophes*. He enumerates certain resemblances between the history of France and the evolution of species of animals. The data of history, he holds, are very similar to the data of paleontology. There are, for instance, the same laws of growth, maturity and senescence, and evolution into a new and more developed species. And he goes on to enumerate five chief cycles in the evolution of France. These are: (1) the conquest of France by the Romans; (2) the invasion of the barbarian hordes, which overthrew and utterly destroyed the Roman power in all of Gaul; (3) the invasion of the Normans; (4) the One Hundred Years' War; and (5) the great World War of 1914. He points out that each of these leading events was a great catastrophe, similar to those recorded in the rocks for animal species. Each cycle occurred at an interval from the catastrophe preceding of about five hundred years or fifteen generations, and from each was born a new era in France. And this, too, is similar to the cycles involved in the evolution of the species. In short, since the invasion of Caesar, five successive Frances can be traced, and this evolution is quite like those separate stages in the evolution of such species as the horse and the elephant.

But now we know that cataclysms among the species are followed by a rejuvenation and a new development. After each one of the cataclysms there is an upward and higher progress. And in the case of the four past cycles in French history this is also known to have happened to France. Therefore, on the basis of this close resemblance, Gautier infers that France can look forward to a new cycle of rejuvenated national energy.

Inasmuch as Spengler's theory and that of Gautier are both based upon false analogies we shall

MONISM VERSUS PLURALISM 197

leave them to cancel each other out. But we must recognize that the cultural pluralism of Spengler is independent of his pessimistic conclusion about the fate of West European civilization. And there is a kernel of profound truth in the theory of cultural pluralism.

4. APPLICATIONS OF CULTURAL MONISM AND PLURALISM TO CURRENT INTERNATIONAL RELATIONS

Many of the cultural monists are ardent defenders of Internationalism. They argue that the goal of human evolution is one world-wide culture, based predominantly upon modern science. To be sure, they use the word science in a broad sense to include the physical, biological, and social sciences, thus making a place for literature, art, and even religion under the third division of science. What they wish to build is a unified humanity in which all men and women will share in the vastly increased store of values made possible by modern science. To achieve this purpose they wish to junk every vestige of individualism within states, as well as every vestige of nationalism in international relations. We must create one supreme super-state so powerful that it will be able to destroy all competition within what are now separate sovereign states as well as all competition between such states. The ethical goal of cultural monism is the creation of a single super-state in the hope that it will hasten that complete socialization of all mankind which the theory of one world-culture demands.

There is something ennobling in working for the unification of all mankind; there is that in this ideal fit to inspire sages and prophets, poets and all lovers of mankind. We must agree with the cultural monists that this really is man's earthly goal. Christianity has always proclaimed that all the kingdoms of this world will ultimately become the kingdom of God here on earth. Judaism and Mohammedanism share this hope with Christianity. And even Buddhism, in its doctrine that Buddha gained his final enlightenment as the result of the working out in human history of a higher world-order, teaches by implication that the goal of humanity is to be a brotherhood of all men and a single world-culture. Johann Gottlieb Fichte, that patriotic but deeply humanitarian German philosopher, finely expressed the profound truth in cultural monism when he wrote: "It is the vocation of our race to unite itself into one single body, all the parts of which shall be thoroughly known to each other, and all possessed of similar culture. . . . Let us ask of history at what period the existing culture has been most widely diffused, and distributed among the greatest number of individuals; and we shall doubtless find that from the beginning of history down to our own day, the few light-points of civilization have spread themselves abroad from their centre, that one individual after another, and one nation after another, has been embraced within their circle, and that this wider outspread of culture is proceeding under our own eyes. And this is the first point to be attained in the endless path of which humanity must advance. Until this shall have been attained, until the existing culture of every age shall have been diffused over the whole inhabited globe, and our race become capable of the most unlimited intercommunication with itself, one nation or one continent must pause on the great common path of progress, and wait for the advance of the others; and each must bring as an offering to the universal commonwealth, for the sake of which alone it exists, its ages of apparent immobility or retrogression. When that first point shall have been attained, when every useful discovery made at one end of the earth shall be at once made known and communicated to all the rest, then, without further interruption, without halt or regress, with united strength and equal step, humanity shall move onward to a higher culture." [6]

However, Fichte had sense enough to know that this goal would not be achieved in a generation. He knew that it would take several eons to complete the process and that men would despair at their labors without the vision of a heavenly kingdom of God now and eternally actual to make that distant hope seem real. And too many contemporary cultural monists, having lost this vision, wish to usher in the brotherhood of man this very night or not later than tomorrow or the day after, and they plan to do it without any reliance on any kind

[6] J. G. Fichte: *The Popular Works of Fichte*, translated by William Smith, Vol. I, pp. 42 f.

of divine guidance. The Marxian materialistic interpretation of history has replaced the Fichtian idealistic interpretation, and this Magog of economic materialism will drive humanity downward instead of pulling it upward. We have dictators enough and to spare within the separate states of the earth today. A super-state controlled by one arch-dictator and several satellites is not likely to commend itself to liberty-loving people. And a super-state that is not so controlled cannot be created tomorrow or the day after. It must grow through centuries. Its process of actualization will perforce be slow.

On the other hand, the cultural pluralists argue that some kind of union of all the states possessing the same culture is the inevitable development of international relations. Pan-Germanism and the general idea of a close federation of English-speaking people are forms of this application of cultural pluralism. In the face of the undeniable fact that several quite distinct cultures hold powerfully entrenched positions on the earth today we are forced to conclude that, at least for the immediate future, liberal thinkers who are deeply interested in promoting the welfare of humanity must adopt cultural pluralism as their working hypothesis. This does not mean that we have to abandon the effort to secure a unified world-order. But it does mean that we must seek this through some such organization as a modified League of Nations. In contrast with the super-state idea of the cultural monists let us designate this type of organization as *cultural federalism*. Those thinkers who defend this position argue that every existing culture has some valuable contribution to make to the enrichment of human life, and that these cultures should create an organization through which they can coöperate to prevent economic materialism and imperialism from ruthlessly destroying what it has taken centuries to produce. We shall develop this idea of cultural federalism more fully in the last two chapters.

What to Read

There is a selection from Oswald Spengler's *Decline of the West* in D. S. Robinson's *Anthology of Recent Philosophy,* pp. 611 ff. See the selections from John Dewey and S. Rhadakrishnan in the same anthology, Part I, Ch. III, and the selections from Hegel (pp. 596 ff.) and Comte (pp. 697 ff.) in the same compiler's *Anthology of Modern Philosophy.* Oswald Spengler's *Man and Technics* is also valuable, and see John Dewey's *Philosophy and Civilization.*

The following important recent works deal with various aspects of the contents of this chapter: J. B. Bury: *The Idea of Progress;* Benedetto Croce: *History: Its Theory and Practice;* George A. Dorsey: *Why We Behave Like Human Beings, The Nature of Man,* and "Race and Civilization," Ch. X of *Whither Mankind,* edited by Charles A. Beard; Glenn Frank: *Thunder and Dawn: the Outlook for Western Civilization with Special Reference to the United States;* Egon Friedell: *A Cultural History of the Modern Age,* 3 vols., translated by C. F. Atkinson; F. H. Giddings: *Civilization and Society;* F. H. Hankins: *The Racial Basis of Civilization: a Critique of the Nordic Doctrine;* Hornell

Hart: *The Technique of Social Progress;* Gerald Heard: *The Emergence of Man;* W. E. Hocking: *The Spirit of World Politics;* A. G. Keller: *Man's Rough Road;* A. L. Kroeber: *Anthropology;* Sir Henry Lambert: *The Nature of History;* J. A. Leighton: *The Individual and the Social Order,* Ch. XXXIII; Robert H. Lowie: *Culture and Ethnology;* R. M. MacIver: *The Modern State,* Ch. X, and *Society: Its Structure and Changes;* Charles H. McIlwain: *The Growth of Political Thought in the West;* R. R. Marett: *Anthropology;* Paul Radin: *The Racial Myth;* James Harvey Robinson: *The Mind in the Making;* Hermann Schneider: *The History of World Civilization from Prehistoric Times to the Middle Ages,* 2 vols., translated by M. M. Green; Albert Schweitzer: *Civilization and Ethics;* Lothrop Stoddard: *The Revolt Against Civilization;* A. M. Tozzer: *Social Origins and Social Continuities;* Clark Wissler: *Man and Culture;* Sir George Young: *The Pendulum of Progress.*

See also Adrian Coates: "A Pluralistic View of History" in *Philosophy,* Vol. VIII, pp. 318-325. The volume entitled *Rethinking Missions* is valuable, especially chapters I-IV, which were written by Professor Hocking.

CHAPTER X

THE MEASURES OF BACKWARDNESS

1. Three Primary Measures of Backwardness

The men of action responsible for the Treaty of Versailles following the World War assumed that there is an essential difference between dominant and subordinate peoples, and that some at least of the subordinate peoples are, and ought to be treated as, culturally backward, whereas they assumed that they themselves were the representatives of progressive peoples. Indeed, the makers of the Treaty even went so far as to ask some of these peoples who had actually served as their allies against the Central Powers, especially certain Islamic groups, to think of themselves as backward. And to enforce this view upon them they gave the people of Syria and Irak a mandate status. Whatever we may think of the treatment accorded the Arabs by the Treaty of Versailles, the question of whether there is an essential distinction between progressive and backward peoples has certainly become acute since the close of the World War. Is this distinction real or fictitious? That is the question we must now consider.

Some anthropologists and students of inter-racial

relations hold that the distinction is a pure fiction which the sovereign states of the earth have found highly useful. They argue that every people may be regarded as superior from some point of view, and that all attempts to rank peoples are purely relative. On the theory that "the mores make anything right" these thinkers have constructed the doctrine that all social orders are morally equal, and that one people is as good and as bad as another.

We cannot accept this theory of universal relativity. It is out of harmony with the spirit of modern life and tends to level all the peoples of the earth down to that of high grade simians. The doctrine of the ethical queerness of states implies that there is a basic distinction between progressive and backward peoples, and we must now attempt to lay down a set of objective tests by which the degree of backwardness of a people can be measured. To be sure, we might adapt the four postulates expounded in Chapter III to this purpose, but since we have already made extensive use of these criteria in evaluating typical actual states we prefer to use other criteria here, leaving it to the reader to apply the postulates of an ideal state. And first let us consider what Professor Hocking has well called the primary measures of backwardness.

(1) *The Mastery of Nature.*—Francis Bacon gave the modern world its shibboleth when he said: "Knowledge is power." By means of the vast increase in scientific knowledge modern men have won an enormously greater control over the forces of

nature. Geological and engineering knowledge enables modern man to utilize a great deal more of the mineral deposits and other natural elements stored up in the earth, and his knowledge of chemistry and physics even enables him to harness the unseen powers of the air and sea. Only recently our knowledge of the hidden energies of men has reached such vast proportions that we have come to use the phrase "human engineering." Modern man has applied this knowledge in creating vast military organizations that threaten the peace of the world. This ability to utilize the natural resources of earth, sea, and air, and the hidden energies of human beings sets modern men apart from the generations of antiquity. But the peoples who have acquired this knowledge, and who have developed the technical skill required in applying it are the beneficiaries. Other peoples of the earth, possessing little or no interest in exploiting natural resources or in applying science to the organization of human society, have not shared so much in such human progress as has been made possible by the increase in scientific knowledge. Consequently, such people really are backward. This is an objective test and it tells a plain tale. A people who cannot use the natural resources of the area of the earth which they occupy are unquestionably a backward people.

(2) *The General Level of Public Morality.*—By public morality here is meant the integrity of all of those who hold positions of responsibility and

authority among a people. This may be discovered *directly* by answering such a question as the following: To what extent does public opinion show an active demand for leaders in all walks of life who have high moral ideals? And it may be discovered *indirectly* by answering the four following questions: (1) How far does the legislative body of the people in question dare go in the enactment of laws that sanction and compel a high moral integrity in all leaders? (2) How far do judges dare go in enforcing such enactments as the legislative body makes? (3) How far do administrators dare go in upholding legislative enactments and judicial decisions? (4) How far do professional recommenders of ideals, such as religious leaders, authors, et cetera, dare go in criticizing the morality of public officials?

There is undoubtedly an exceedingly high correlation between the cultural evolution of any people, and the morality of those who have the responsibilities of leadership. Negatively this is expressed by the amount of crime there is among the people, and the degree of success with which criminals are hunted down and punished. If public officials are permitted to wink an eye at crime, then the people ruled by such officials are a backward people. Positively the general level of public morality is determined by the extent to which all officials are active in working for the general welfare. A people which can develop leaders who administer whatever function is entrusted to them under a sense of responsibility, and who are of such high integrity that they are not corruptible by bribery are a progressive people. Even though morality is largely a personal matter, this test is in fact objective. "By their fruits ye shall know them" is a saying especially true of public officials, since their deeds are always more or less in the limelight.

(3) *The Condition of the Masses.*—A third primary measure of backwardness is the condition of the masses of the population. If the vast majority of the population are in dire want for the necessities of life, if the wealth of the State is concentrated in the hands of a very small minority, if cultural advantages and educational facilities are withheld from all except the privileged classes, a people must be judged to be backward. Referring to this as "the most patent and reliable of all tests" Professor Hocking points out that it is really a corollary of the other two measures. He writes: "The presumption is that, if the economic problem has been well and scientifically faced in any community, the common people will not be in misery,—dirty, diseased, threatened at every change of season with famine. And, if the moral problem has likewise been met, the common people will be decently educated, indisposed to crime, free of mind and capable of adding something to the intelligence of government." [1]

These three primary measures of backwardness

---

[1] From W. E. Hocking: *The Spirit of World Politics,* p. 16, by permission of The Macmillan Company, Publishers.

are genuine objective tests. They enable us to classify the peoples of the earth according to the degree of their backwardness. But they are heavily weighted in favor of the peoples making up Western civilization. And this lays them open to the charge that they are merely our prejudices and that they have no validity outside of West European culture. Doubtless many defenders of Islamic, Hindu, Chinese, and Japanese cultures would seriously question the universal validity of these three measures.

2. Cultural Latency

In consistency with our previous theory that the cultural order is higher than the private and the public order and is the ultimate reason for their existence, let us attempt to use it as a measure of backwardness. Let us evaluate the various peoples in terms of the cultural values which they have contributed and of the cultural fertility that is latent in them. This measure Professor Hocking calls *cultural latency*.

In Yucatan there still exists a remnant of the descendants of the old Mayan people who created the Mayan culture now being studied by trained American archaeologists. Those who study these later-day Mayans find no evidence that they have any capacity to appreciate what their ancestors produced, or any creative urge within them to perpetuate and enhance the cultural values of the people from whom they have descended. Such a people must be ranked as decadent. There is no hope of

MEASURES OF BACKWARDNESS

their ever being able to rejuvenate their culture. They may later interbreed with other immigrant peoples until a virile race is produced which is capable of another organized communal life out of which a new culture will arise. But measured by the standard of cultural latency the contemporary Mayan people are not any longer capable of preserving and enhancing the cultural values of the people from whom they descended. Mayan culture exists only in the form of ruins and vestigial customs that are practiced by these decadent representatives of it. These representatives do not even understand what their ancestors created. American archaeologists have had to recover the existing remains of the great Mayan culture which flourished in Yucatan many centuries ago.

On the other hand, the Arabian people, who have descended from those who produced the great Islamic culture that swept over the near East and into the Balkans and Spain from the eighth century of our era onward, and then gradually declined, have preserved many of the cultural values of their progenitors. Moreover, they show many evidences of a latent power to create new cultural values which will enhance the work already done in the centuries of the past. Islamic culture is not dead and it is not decadent. It is merely dormant. There is every reason to believe that it is again becoming active and that it will add new values to those it has already produced. Measured by the standard of cultural latency the Arabian people must be given a much higher rank than the present-day descendants of the ancient Mayan people.

This is a measure of backwardness that is independent of the three primary measures and which does enable us to rank some existing cultures higher than others, yes, in some respects higher even than our own boasted Western civilization. Today, Professor Hocking tells us, "over all the Orient, there broods this sense of *latency,* of an immense and unfathomed capacity for new life, the potency of something radically different from our type, if it can be given its own time and mode of growth. We have no need to deal fearfully with the 'mystery of the Orient,' but we have every reason for dealing respectfully with qualities which, varying as they do from ours, give promise of still other variants, not poisonous and weird, but noble, humane, and also universal." [2] And many would agree with him in the opinion: "I am ready to say that, even now, there are many respects, as in grace of life, dignity of thought and language, courtesy, hospitality, conversation, intuitive poetry and metaphysical sense, in which it is we who are the backward peoples." [3] And he goes on to enumerate such qualities as the *power to wait*—"a persistent sense of the eternal element in change, a background and cure for the dizziness of unmitigated flux" which gives their social order a stability ours lacks; and a keen sense of the personal element in such impersonal affairs

[2] *Loco citato,* p. 34.
[3] *Loco citato,* p. 31.

as science and law. When measured by the standards of cultural latency who knows that Western culture is superior to that of Arabia or India or China? One thing is certain, the earth belongs to those peoples who have cultural latency, whose cultural possibilities have not all been realized. What if we have mastered nature, created law and order, and made the masses more comfortable with radios, telephones, automobiles, and numerous other machines and instruments of human comfort, if our spiritual life becomes so cramped that we produce no original art, or other cultural values? To the extent that we fail culturally we are backward, even though we claim to be progressive. In the long run the true measure of the worth of a people is their ability to conserve and to enhance their cultural values.

There is an important principle implicit in this measure of cultural latency, namely, that a poorly governed but self-governed people have a better chance of actualizing their latent cultural possibilities than a well-governed people whose affairs are administered by alien officials. This principle is especially important in determining whether a backward people should be made dependent on a progressive people, since it follows from it that the presumption is in favor of leaving as much control in the hands of natives as they are able to exercise. We will discuss this matter more fully in the next chapter when we take up the rights of backward peoples. Here it is only necessary to explain why this principle is implied in the measure of cultural latency.

Alien control over a people has a retarding effect on their creative energies. It amounts to a form of slavery. Although the alien government may give complete freedom to each individual living under their régime, the group as a whole is restrained from developing along the line of its own genius. Their cultural activities are no longer spontaneous and their zeal for their own philosophy, music, architecture, and literature is dampened by the presence among them of officials representing another culture which claims superiority over their own. The citizen of such a state who would be most likely to contribute to its culture is forced into the position of having to adapt himself to an alien rule and this tends to destroy his urge to creativity. He loses heart and principle, because of the ever present need of accommodating himself to the alien régime. He feels himself to be a man without a country, he can command no respect from those whom he serves, an inferiority complex is developed in him by the unnaturalness of the situation in which he is placed, and at best he becomes a tamed cynic or a cunning deceiver.

In *The Native's Return* Louis Adamic has well described the effect of five hundred years of Turkish domination of the Serbs. He quotes a Croat he met in Belgrade as saying: "The Serbs were in political and economic bondage to the Turks for five hundred years—unwillingly, of course, with all the

MEASURES OF BACKWARDNESS

inner power of resistance that is characteristic of them. . . . They were physically helpless against their brutal masters and exploiters. They were deprived of all human and legal rights. Their one defense was *podvala*—cunning, deceit—which they practiced against their oppressors through the centuries until recently, when circumstances made it possible for them to liberate themselves; but meanwhile cunning has become an art with them and part of their nature."

In such creative work as is done by the most gifted individuals in a culture that is dominated by alien officials, these effects are subtly expressed. There is a plaintiveness in their music, a note of sorrow and longing in their poetry, a tragedy in their sagas, a pessimistic moan in their philosophy.[4] Referring to the Kossovo epic of the Serbian people, their greatest literary production, the Croat quoted above continues: "Their Kossovo epic . . . was a form of *podvala*. They fooled the Turks. The Turks didn't know what these songs and legends really meant even when they understood the words. They probably thought the Serbs were a little crazy to glorify their defeat. . . . In my mind, the Kossovo epic is first of all a piece of great political subtlety —a bit of colossal propaganda, cunning as any-

[4] A highly educated negro, who read this chapter, wrote me the following comment on this sentence: "I am reminded here of many (a very large percentage) of the spirituals, poems, stories, and sayings of the American negro. There is no doubt but that they are eloquent illustrations of the truthfulness of this statement. They are probably the best examples to be found in large mass in the world's literature, present or past."

thing."[5] Thus such cultural values as are created by a politically enslaved people reflect the status of foreign domination. Remove this domination and a people with cultural latency will recover their interest in conserving and enhancing their spiritual heritage and there will be a cultural renaissance among that people. This explains why it is preferable for a people to govern themselves, even though they do it poorly, than for them to be better governed by alien officials not of their own choosing.

3. OTHER MEASURES OF BACKWARDNESS

A distinguished anthropologist, the Dutchman H. Ten Kate, prepared a table entitled *Distribution of Some Characteristics of Highest Civilization* in which he ranked the following eleven countries: Great Britain, Northern France, the Netherlands, Germany, Switzerland, Italy, the United States, Mexico, Argentina, Paraguay, and Japan, according to their degree of backwardness. He used twelve characteristics of the highest value to humanity as criteria. These are: (1) power of initiative, (2) inventiveness and capacity for formulating new ideas, (3) power to lead and control other races,

[5] Louis Adamic: *The Native's Return*, p. 249. (Harpers) Compare John Dewey: "It is significant that many words for intelligence suggest the idea of circuitous, evasive activity—often with a sort of intimation of even moral obliquity. The bluff, hearty man goes straight (and stupidly, it is implied) at some work. The intelligent man is cunning, shrewd (crooked), wily, subtle, crafty, artful, designing—the idea of indirection is involved. An idea is a method of evading, circumventing, or surmounting through reflection obstacles that otherwise would have to be attacked by brute force."—*How We Think*, Revised ed., p. 135 (D. C. Heath & Co.).

MEASURES OF BACKWARDNESS

(4) ability to carry out far-reaching enterprises covering long periods and areas, (5) application of principles of hygiene, (6) degree of personal safety, (7) standard of honesty and morality, (8) highly developed system of education, (9) ability to develop philosophical systems, (10) sense for beauty in the plastic arts including architecture, (11) sense for beauty in literature (belles-lettres), and (12) sense for beauty in nature (flowers, scenery, etc.). These are obviously similar to the four measures already discussed. Thus criteria 1-5 may all be included under the mastery of nature, 6-7 under public morality, 8 under condition of the masses, and 9-12 under cultural latency.[6] Mr. Ten Kate used each of these twelve criteria to rank each of the eleven countries mentioned above, and he found that Great Britain, Germany, and the Netherlands ranked highest, Mexico, Argentina, and Paraguay lowest, with the United States and Northern France in the upper middle group, and Switzerland, Japan, and Italy in the lower middle group.

Two American anthropologists, Professors Griffith Taylor and R. B. Dixon have attempted to determine the difference between progressive and backward people by means of head measurements. They argue that the form of the head is more distinctive than any other human characteristic. Backward peoples are those having long, narrow, and low

[6] Mr. Ten Kate's table has been published in Professor Ellsworth Huntington's *Civilization and Climate,* p. 160 (Yale University Press, 1915).

heads with little brain capacity. Progressive peoples are those having round heads because such a head can hold the largest brain in proportion to its surface and weight. There are six head types in between the long-narrow-low type and the most perfect round type. When the peoples of the world are studied in the light of head types it is found that the most backward peoples have been pushed back to the margins of each continent or to regions of the earth protected by mountains, tropical forestry, or in some other way, whereas the better portions of the earth are occupied by round-headed types. These anthropologists have worked this theory out in great detail and have applied it to explain the various waves of immigration of peoples during the long period of pre-history as well as during historic times. They both agree that the present apparent racial inferiority of some peoples of the earth and superiority of other peoples is purely accidental. They use other measurements besides head measurements, but they consider head measurements to be the most reliable.[7]

To the extent that this measure of backwardness would explain all cultural differences by bone anatomy it is obviously a one-sided view. And yet

---

[7] See Griffith Taylor: *The Evolution and Distribution of Race, Culture, and Language,* New York, 1921; and R. B. Dixon: *The Racial History of Man,* New York, 1923. There is an excellent summary of these books in Ellsworth Huntington's *The Character of Races,* Chapters VI, VII. See also Dr. Taylor's article entitled: "Environment and Nation" in the *American Journal of Sociology,* Vol. XC, pp. 21-34, and his article entitled: "The Ecological Basis of Anthropology" in *Ecology,* Vol. XV, pp. 223-242.

it is valuable in showing that progressiveness is not a fixed characteristic, but is so variable that a people may be progressive in one age and become backward later. And it also shows that the problem of the relations of progressive to backward peoples are enormously complicated by reason of the fact that every extensive region of the earth contains a population in which there are a number of different racial strata, some of which are more progressive than others. Think, for example, of the Philippine Islands. Nevertheless the relations of these various strata to each other should be based upon ethical principles, as we will attempt to show in the next chapter.

Another possible measure of backwardness is the degree to which the internal social organizations controlling the customs of the masses tend towards rigidity and fixity. Think, for example, of the people of Thibet. Here we have a unique type of theocratic social order. Every male child born in a family and growing to maturity, except one, is required to become a Lama, this being the name of the celibate monk in Thibet. The supreme head of the Lamaseries of Thibet, the Grand Lama of one of the Lamaseries near Lhasa, is the ruler of the country. A social structure of this kind weakens the virility and fertility of a people to such an extent that it condemns them to a permanent condition of backwardness. On the other hand, a people having a flexible internal social organization can advance and usually do so sooner or later. It may be that the most backward peoples of the earth have become so because of the heavy yoke of custom upon them. In some cases this undoubtedly leads to the slow but relentless decadence which marks a people who have lost their creative urge and are in danger of sinking back into barbarism. For the decadence of a culture is worse than mere backwardness.

However, internal social organization is so closely tied up with religion and with the private and personal beliefs of the individual members of a culture that it is difficult to formulate it so that it can be used as a measure of backwardness. Every people seems to be a law unto itself so far as the general form of its folkways are concerned. Only in such an extreme case as Lamaism are we really able to evaluate a people by the use of this principle. And in such a case we probably have actual decadence rather than backwardness.

4. A Provisional Classification of Peoples

The men of action classified the peoples disposed of in the Treaty of Versailles on the basis of the primary measures of backwardness, arranging them into the following groups:

I. *The A Mandates*—those peoples that are least backward—Palestine, Syria, and Iraq.
II. *The B Mandates*—those more backward but ultimately capable of self-government—former German African Colonies.

III. *The C Mandates*—those judged permanently incapable of self-government—the Pacific Islands mandated to Japan.

Over against these were the nations admitted to the League of Nations, all of which were regarded as progressive peoples. This classification could be extended to all the peoples of the earth, but it would not be satisfactory since it is purely artificial.

Professor Ellsworth Huntington deserves great credit for having secured the coöperation of approximately one hundred and fifty expert anthropologists, ethnologists, and geographers in ranking all the various races now extant on the earth. His method was to secure answers to an extensive questionnaire from competent judges belonging to different races and motivated by different ideals. Describing this method, he writes: "In the autumn of 1913 I asked over two hundred people in twenty-seven countries to help in preparing a map. Most fortunately this was before the great war broke out. Good feeling prevailed everywhere, and among men of sound judgment there was perhaps as little racial prejudice as at any time during the course of history. This is especially important because similar conditions may not prevail again for years.

"The persons whose assistance was asked were selected for various reasons. The larger number were geographers whose first duty is to know all parts of the world. Ethnologists in considerable numbers were included for the same reason, but they responded less freely than the geographers. Historians, diplomats, colonial officials, travelers, missionaries, editors, educators, and business men were all included. The only criterion was that each person should possess an extensive knowledge of the world through personal knowledge, or, in a few cases, through reading. Some were selected because of knowledge of special regions not well known to most people and only reached by extensive travel." [8]

On the basis of the answers which he secured from those who responded to his questionnaire, Professor Huntington has constructed a set of tables containing detailed ratings of all the peoples of the earth. And he has also prepared a number of interesting maps to show graphically the distribution of civilization on the earth. His work is based on the theory that climate is the controlling factor in this distribution, and it must be taken into account by all who attempt to classify the peoples of the earth in the future.

What is greatly needed is a careful study by some International Commission, possibly under the supervision of the League of Nations, of all the peoples of the earth with a view to determining the exact status of each culturally. Such a study should be made by experts, not in the sense of an international brain trust, but in the sense that each member should be a trained ethnologist, capable of applying in an unprejudiced manner the latest methods of determin-

---

[8] See Ellsworth Huntington: *Civilization and Climate*, Yale Press, Chapter VIII, pp. 148-182, and Appendices, pp. 297-314.

MEASURES OF BACKWARDNESS

ing the cultural level of a people. And an effort should be made to get the various progressive peoples of the earth to agree on the classification resulting from such a scientific study, and to adopt common methods of administering such backward peoples as are committed to their care. This preliminary work is the indispensable condition of the development of a genuinely ethical treatment of backward peoples. Until this is accomplished political ethics, so far as the relations between backward and progressive peoples are concerned, will remain unscientific and largely speculative. We cannot determine how a progressive people should treat a backward people until we have definite knowledge of the stage or degree of backwardness of that people. As long as progressive states keep their own citizens, and those of other progressive states, in the dark on this matter they will be able to justify whatever treatment they care to mete out to the backward people committed to their charge. Although the task we are here suggesting might take fifty years to complete it is an enterprise worthy of highly civilized people, and eventually it will be accomplished. And when it is, a great step forward will have been taken in that division of political ethics which deals with the relations between progressive and backward peoples. Most civilized people have ways of preventing domestic animals from being mistreated. Why should there not be an International Humane Society to protect backward people from oppression?

There is, however, a danger in making such a cultural classification as has just been suggested. Think of the abuses to which it would be liable! Just as there have been many vicious uses made of the results achieved in psychological and educational testing, instead of their being used to the advantage for which they were intended or not being used at all, so it could be with a scientifically accurate cultural classification of peoples. Just as some teachers are guilty of using I. Q., E. Q., M. A. and E. A. to excuse their own poor teaching efficiency, and just as school boards often use these data to justify their failure to provide for the proper education of *all* of the children of their community, so the mandatory power administering a backward people's affairs might use the very fact of an officially agreed status of such a people to justify its vicious rule or guardianship over them. Hence, even though such a classification as was suggested above were made, the need of enlightened and ever-present supervision of the administration of the affairs of every backward people would still exist. But all this assumes that backward people have rights, and to that question we must now turn.

What to Read

The text of the Treaty of Versailles has been edited with notes by H. W. V. Temperley, under the title *The Treaty of Peace,* with an Introduction by Lord R. Cecil. See the concise analysis of its provisions in the article entitled "Versailles, Treaty of" in the 14th ed. of the *Encyclopedia Bri-*

tannica. See also H. W. V. Temperley, editor: *History of the Peace Conference,* 6 vols.; K. F. Nowak: *Versailles* (English translation); H. Stegemann: *The Mirage of Versailles;* and A. Tardieu: *The Truth About the Treaty.*

There is a valuable article entitled "Ethnology" in Hastings' *Encyclopedia of Religion and Ethics,* which gives an interesting conspectus of all of the races of man and an indication of the chief cultural differences. There are also the following important articles: "Anthropology," "Anthropology Applied," "Comparative Ethics," and "Races of Mankind," in the 14th edition of the *Encyclopedia Britannica.* See also the classic work of F. Ratzel: *History of Mankind* (English translation); and that by E. B. Tylor: *Anthropology.* J. G. Frazer's *The Golden Bough* is a storehouse of information about the lower races of man.

In addition to Professor Ellsworth Huntington's books cited in the footnotes to this chapter, see his recently published textbook entitled *Social and Economic Geography.*

Other valuable references are: *Bureau of American Ethnology* Bulletin No. 30 (by various authors); A. C. Haddon: *The Races of Man;* Alexander Goldenweiser: *History, Psychology, and Culture;* J. R. Kantor: *Principles of Psychology,* 2 vols. (see especially Vol. I, pp. 167 ff., and 197 ff.) and *An Outline of Social Psychology,* Ch. IV; A. H. Keane: *Man: Past and Present;* G. H. Lane-Fox Pitt-Rivers: *The Clash of Culture and the Contact of Races;* W. H. R. Rivers: *Ethnology and Psychology,* and *Social Organization;* G. Eliot Smith: *The Evolution of Man;* and H. W. Wilder: *The Pedigree of the Human Race.*

See also the references at the end of the preceding chapter and those at the end of the following chapter.

CHAPTER XI

THE RIGHTS OF BACKWARD PEOPLES

1. The Right of Conquest

Political realists usually take it for granted that the relations of a progressive to a backward people are determined wholly by force. By this they mean the conquering power which a progressive people have over a backward people by virtue of their superior mastery over the forces of nature, as this is expressed in their military strength. This conquering power may exist by being actually exerted, as when the American colonists gradually extended their control over the regions of North America formerly occupied by various Indian tribes. In this case the backward peoples were actually conquered by the progressive people. But conquering power may be merely implicit as in the case of the relation of the people of the United States to the people of Mexico *now*. To be sure, there was a Mexican War in which territory was wrested from Mexico by the overt exercise of conquering power. And the punitive expedition sent into Mexico by President Woodrow Wilson was also a case of the actual use of the conquering power of a progressive people. Yet our conquering power over Mexico today exists as something unused, but which on occasion could be used. It is implied but not exercised. No one can doubt the reality of this power providing there should arrive a real necessity for exercising it. The Mexican people *could be* conquered by the people of the United States.

The question we now have to raise is: Does a progressive people have an ethical right to conquer a backward people, and, if so, does that right come from the power to conquer? To put it differently, does the right arise from and depend upon the power to conquer, or does it come into existence only as a result of the actual consummation of this conquering? Did the Japanese have a right to go into Manchuria because they had conquering power enough to do it? Did the fact that they conquered it create whatever rights they now have there? These are crucial questions which have to be answered, if we are to reach a satisfactory theory of the rights of peoples. It is a form of the old problem of whether *might makes right*.

The actual fighting which ends in a complete subjugation of one people by another does not make right. Unless right already exists the fighting cannot possibly create it. For it is a basic ethical principle that every right implies a duty, and a right created by fighting would be a right which carried no obligation with it. This theory that right comes from conquering power gives all of the rights to the progressive people and concedes none to those who do not have conquering power. Suppose one nation in the world should become so powerful that it could conquer all other peoples of the earth. On the theory that might makes right this state and its citizens could acquire all the rights of all mankind simply by conquering. The act of conquering would establish a world order in which one people only would have rights, and all other peoples, having been conquered, would possess no rights. And such a tyrannical condition of human affairs would have to be judged ethical, if right is created by fighting, that is, by the actual exercise of conquering power. So we must reject the theory that right is created by conquest. If the colonists had a right to conquer the Indians, then they had it before they conquered them. If the United States had a right to conquer Mexico in the Mexican War, the victory in that war did not create that right. And if the right existed prior to the war, its source cannot be the actual conquest.

Does it, then, come from the existence of the power to conquer? Shall we say that it is always right for the stronger to control the weaker? Can right be derived from mere conquering power? No. This must be the answer if we are to maintain our position that all peoples have rights. For such a theory also makes right wholly one-sided. Only the progressive peoples as determined by the power to master nature would have rights, if right comes from conquering power. This would create a monstrous upsetting of the principle of moral symmetry. A right must be something which all reasoning persons can acknowledge. And no reasoning person, not a member of the state possessing conquering power, could acknowledge the right of a state possessing it to conquer his people. The right must have some other source than conquering power. Whatever rights the American people have over against the Indians or the Mexicans must be derived from some other source than their conquering power. Whatever rights the Japanese have over against the people of Manchuria must have another basis than conquering power. The theory of "a right of conquest," the theory that all rights of one people in relation to another people arises either from actual conquest or from conquering power which can be used whether it really is or not, is a theory which is equivalent to a denial of any *ethical right* so far as the relations of peoples to each other are concerned.

2. Economic Imperialism

The men of action responsible for the making of the Versailles Treaty rejected the old idea that might makes right when they adopted the *mandate idea* as a principle of disposing of backward peoples. For this idea implies that a backward people have *some rights,* and that a progressive people who administer the affairs of a backward people have certain obligations toward these people. At least this does mark a distinct advance in the development of a world conscience towards backward peoples. And there are other evidences that such a conscience has been developing. Here in the United States a much more humane attitude toward the remaining tribes of Indians has developed. This is proven by the fact that in recent years deliberate efforts to preserve the Indian cultures have been made. Likewise England and France have taken a serious interest in the native cultures that were committed to their care in the earlier history of colonial expansion, and their scientific research on these cultures has been and is of inestimable value to mankind. Moreover, they are adopting the policy of sending into their colonies only administrators who have been given a thorough training, which includes a detailed knowledge of the native culture over which they are to exercise authority. These facts prove that some of the most progressive peoples, in the sense of those possessing the greatest mastery over nature and the greatest military strength, are now committed to the view that backward peoples do have certain rights which their alien governors must respect. Consequently the principle that might makes right in international relations has been or is being abandoned.

What is taking its place? In actual practice what is the theory that dominates the treatment of backward peoples by progressive peoples today? Let us call the theory of the men of action who are in control of world affairs *economic imperialism*. What theory of the rights of peoples is implied in this theory? We can best answer this question by summarizing in four basic propositions the essence of this

RIGHTS OF BACKWARD PEOPLES

theory. These propositions express the idea of the men of action as to the rights of backward people.

(1) *Backward People Ought to be Unfree and Dependent.*—It was taken for granted by the makers of the Versailles Treaty that being backward means being in a condition of dependence on some progressive people. This dependence was treated as a necessary corollary of backwardness. Nature having been unfriendly to certain peoples, by making them what they are and producing them where they are, and friendly to certain other peoples in these respects, why should statesmen not regard the actual *status quo* as sufficient proof that nature intended that every backward people should be unfree and dependent upon some progressive people? Thus this proposition seems to be a kind of law of nature. Sometimes it is dignified by the name of *manifest destiny* and is used as a moral principle to justify any mistreatment of native peoples by alien invaders.

(2) *The World's Economic Resources Belong to Those Who Know How to Use Them.*—If there exist anywhere on earth mineral deposits or other natural resources, and the territory where they exist is occupied by a backward people, who do not even know of their existence and who would not have the technical skill to utilize them even though they did know of their existence, then these resources rightly belong to those who have the explorative genius to ferret them out, and the engineering skill to make them available for human consumption or human

use. For nature's resources belong to men in proportion to their ability to use them. This, too, seems to be a kind of a law of nature.

(3) *The Destruction of Cultures to the Extent that They Interfere with This Exploitation.*—In exploiting natural resources, in making them serve the ends of those who can use them, it is justifiable to destroy the existing cultures of the peoples now occupying the region of the earth where these resources are. Native cultures have no rights that conflict with the principle of economic exploitation. For that is a natural right that belongs to progressive people by virtue of the actual fact of their progressiveness. Whenever it is necessary for a progressive people to destroy a native culture in the interest of the exploitation of natural resources, then such destruction is right. Otherwise it is wrong.

(4) *The Goal of Humanity Is a Uniform Planetary Civilization Built upon a Scientific Foundation.*—This proposition buttresses the third. Only by a full exploitation of all of the earth's natural resources can the destiny of the human race be fulfilled. This destiny is the creation of a uniform planetary civilization, based upon the application of a knowledge of the laws of nature to a complete control over the forces of nature. As humanity moves forward to a realization of the most complete mastery of nature conceivable, separate cultures must give way to the onward march of science. Here is a special application of the idea of cultural

monism which was explained above. The right to destroy those native cultures that hinder the progress of mankind toward a uniform planetary civilization is deduced from that idea.

These four propositions are the ethical implications of the dogma of economic imperialism. What is to be said about this dogma? Does it give an adequate basis for an ethical theory of the rights of peoples?

This dogma is refuted by the ethically sound principle: *"There can be no power-over without power-for."* [1] This is a fundamental ethical principle in all personal relations. I have no right to use other persons for my own ends. In all of my relations I must be a person and respect others as persons. Kant and Hegel and their followers have made this principle fundamental in all personal ethical relations. And it is also the basic principle of the social ethics of the new humanism shared by such realists as Bertrand Russell and Roy Wood Sellars and such pragmatists as John Dewey and William James. Stated in positive form it would be: Assuming and exercising power-over others entails the obligation to use such power for the betterment of those over whom it is exercised.

Now this principle can and must be extended to

[1] This is Professor Hocking's principle. He writes: "Power in the form of science flows out through education, and through all forms of communicating ideas. The centers of knowledge exert a silent and universal sort of power known as 'authority': they have power *over* men by first having power *for* them." *The Spirit of World Politics*, p. 502. Reprinted by permission of The Macmillan Co., Publishers.

cultures. Believe in and work for the enhancement of your own culture, but respect the other cultures of the world—this should be the moral maxim of every civilized person. As a citizen of the United States it is my privilege and my duty to work for the enhancement of the new culture that is evolving in the Western hemisphere, but it remains my duty to respect all other cultures. And since this is my duty it is also the duty of my country. My country has no right to exploit the mineral resources of Mexico unless it use this power-over for the good of the Mexican people. This principle is the very essence of an ethical attitude.

Economic imperialism ignores, if it does not flaunt, this principle. It demands that a people, who accept this principle in their dealings as a group with other progressive peoples, should abandon it when they deal with backward peoples. And this would imply that it should be abandoned when a civilized man meets a savage or a man from a lower culture. The truth is that no progressive people have a right to exercise power over a backward people unless they accept the obligation to use that power for the betterment of that people. The so-called right to economic exploitation, if it exists at all, carries with it a duty to conserve the culture of the people occupying the territory that is being exploited.

Our conclusion, then, is that reason cannot recognize any right to power-over which excludes the obligation to use that power for the good of those over whom it is exercised. The right of economic exploitation, interpreted so as to give all the benefits to the exploiters, is an ethical myth—a fiction invented by those political realists who believe in one people taking everything they can get. It is a nationalistic form of rationalization carried out to salve the world-conscience of that nation which practices economic exploitation. But that world-conscience will continue to function and to grow until it forces upon civilized nations a full recognition of the rights of backward peoples. A few centuries hence the theory of economic imperialism will be treated by all mankind for what it is, the wolfish doctrine that might makes right dressed up in sheep's clothing. We return, then, to our basic quest for the real source of the rights of peoples.

3. Cultural Values the Basis of Right

A theory of the rights of peoples which starts from the assumption that backward peoples' rights are wholly subordinate to the rights of progressive people is one-sided and false. We must start with the assumption that the fact of the existence on the earth of a culture is in itself a sufficient basis for a theory of the rights of the people who have inherited that culture. For they have a duty to preserve the cultural values that have been transmitted to them by their ancestors, and this duty carries with it a correlative right to the preservation of their culture. And if they have the duty to preserve their culture they also have the duty to enrich and enhance it as far as possible. Consequently, they also have the right to develop their own culture along the line of their own genius. No other people can do this for them, and therefore all other people should respect their right to do it for themselves. In other words, the right of a people to conserve their own cultural values, and their right to create new cultural values that are compatible with those transmitted to them are two rights which certainly belong to every people that exists on the earth today with a communal life sufficiently organized to prove the existence of a cultural solidarity. And it is the duty of every progressive people to acknowledge and to respect these two rights of every backward people. For these two rights are inherent in the cultural existence of the backward peoples.

They are in no sense derivative from the conquering or exploitive power of the progressive people who happen to be in a temporary position of superiority to that backward people.

To illustrate, the American people took over from Spain the sovereignty over the people of the Philippine archipelago. Whether they secured this right to govern these people by purchase, or by conquering the Spaniards, or by treaty is here of no consequence. For whatever rights the United States may have there do not in any way destroy or mitigate the importance of the prior rights of the Filipino people to preserve and enhance their own culture. For those rights were there before we took over the sovereignty, and they are independent of whatever rights we may have to govern the people.

Do these two cultural rights carry with them a third basic right, namely, the right of every people to self-determination? Have the people of the Philippine Islands a right to determine their own destiny without any interference or guidance whatsoever from the United States? We discussed in the preceding chapter the principle that a poorly governed but self-governed people is more likely to develop and expand culturally than one ruled by an alien people. It follows from that principle that every people should have the right of self-determination to the degree that it is possible for them to govern themselves. The less alien rule the better. Yet alien rule may be necessary and when it is the right to complete self-determination is set aside. What are the conditions that should exist, if a people are to be given the right of self-government?

(1) The progressive peoples of the earth have a right to demand of a backward people that they manage the territory they occupy and utilize its natural resources reasonably well. When this condition is not met the territory in question and its natural resources are made useless, if not positively harmful. And in the face of the enormous increase in the population of the earth, and the myriad of elemental human needs that are unsatisfied no backward people have a right to reserve a sizeable portion of the globe merely for their happy hunting ground. Their leaders must be able to demon-

strate to the world that this territory and its resources are being intelligently managed.

(2) A backward people cannot expect their right to self-determination to be recognized by progressive peoples unless they demonstrate their ability to govern themselves well enough not to be a menace to their neighbors. It is no longer possible for the advanced nations of the earth to tolerate anarchic conditions anywhere on the globe. Such areas must be policed and controlled so that they may not become infested with brigands and bandits that prey upon all civilized peoples. A people that are unable to govern themselves must be governed in the interest of the general welfare of humanity.

(3) Nor is it any longer possible to let any people of the earth live in absolute isolation from the rest of the world. Progressive peoples have a right to force, if necessary, any backward or decadent people to carry on international relations with them. If they cannot do this with a fair degree of competency they must be subjected to as much alien rule or compulsion as is necessary to bring this about.

Thus, while acknowledging the right of every backward people to preserve and to enhance their own culture, we can concede the right to self-determination only to those peoples who demonstrate their capacity for self-government by meeting these three elemental conditions. When they fail to meet these conditions they forfeit their right to self-government temporarily, but they do not lose their right to preserve and to enhance their own cultural values. And a progressive people, assuming the rôle of governor of a backward people, commits a great injustice whenever they use their position to root out the indigenous culture and to replace it with their own. But who is to determine whether a given people are meeting the three conditions, and whether the actions of the alien governors are unjust? If every people has a *prima facie* right to self-determination, and if a given people only forfeit it by demonstrating their failure to meet the conditions specified, it is essential to define a definite way of determining when a people need to be governed by an alien people, and what alien people in particular are to assume the governorship.

4. How the Right to Self-Government Is to Be Determined

The fact that a people has the actual status of being incapable of self-government carries with it the implication that such a people are not able to determine when they need guidance from an alien people. Certain of their enlightened leaders may think that self-government is possible, but they are likely to be mistaken. Moreover, these leaders may be actuated by self-interest rather than by genuinely patriotic motives. This has often been the case, and when it is, the proof that such a people need alien guidance is greatly strengthened. We may lay down the basic negative generalization:

No backward people are capable of judging whether they have the capacity for self-government.

On the other hand, this must be balanced by another negative generalization that is equally important: *No progressive people, whose major interests are affected, are capable of judging whether a backward people in whose territory they are interested are capable of self-government.* This principle is necessary to exclude the theory that might makes right, and to prevent the exploitation of a backward people by some neighboring progressive people. From an ethical point of view it is wrong for a strong military power to bully a weak and inferior people. And it is even worse for them to presume to dominate the internal policies of a weaker people, on the pretext that their own vital interests demand that they be given control over the destinies of that people.

It follows that the right of a backward people to govern themselves must be determined by those progressive peoples not especially interested in the territory. Whenever the question of the future status of a backward people becomes acute, *all* of the existing progressive peoples of the world must investigate the conditions and give a hearing to all interested parties, after which they must decide whether and to what extent that backward people requires alien guidance or control. Having done this, they may also select one of their number and charge that state with the obligation of administering such guidance or control as is necessary. Or

RIGHTS OF BACKWARD PEOPLES

they may create an international commission to which this responsibility shall be given. Whatever arrangement may be made it is essential that all of the progressive peoples hold that state or commission to which this obligation is intrusted responsible for the manner in which it is carried out. In this way justice can be done to the backward people, as well as to all interested progressive peoples. Inasmuch as this solution of the problem of who shall determine the right of a people to self-government involves some sort of joint action on the part of all progressive peoples, the question arises as to whether this would not require an organization of world powers similar to the League of Nations. We shall discuss that question more at length in the next chapter.

Here it is sufficient to point out the way in which the civilized peoples of the earth must coöperate together in the building of ethical international relations. A recent illustration will make the matter clearer. In April of 1934 the Japanese Government announced to the world that no other power would be permitted to deal directly with China, without first consulting with the Japanese Government. This action was interpreted as being equivalent to a Japanese Monroe Doctrine for China and Eastern Asia. In replying to this expressed position of the Japanese Government, the President of the United States, through his Secretary of State, issued an official declaration giving expression to the theory of the rights of peoples, which contained the following statements: "In the international associations and relationships of the United States, the American government seeks to be duly considerate of the rights, the obligations and the legitimate interests of other countries, and it expects on the part of other governments due consideration of the rights, the obligations and the legitimate interests of the United States.

"In the opinion of the American People and the American government, no nation can, without the assent of the other nations concerned, rightfully endeavor to make conclusive its will in situations where there are involved the rights, the obligations and the legitimate interests of other sovereign states.

"The American government has dedicated the United States to the policy of the good neighbor and to the practical application of that policy it will continue, on its own part and in association with other governments, to devote its best efforts."

These statements lay down the fundamental principle that no one progressive people has the right to dictate what the relations of a backward people shall be to other progressive peoples. By implication they mean that these rights must be determined by the coöperation of all the nations concerned, and in our day that can only mean all the nations of the earth, since every world power is today affected by whatever major happening may occur anywhere on the earth. Of course the statements quoted actually refer to the Nine Power Pact dealing with the relations of China to eight other world powers. But it is legitimate to extend the principle to include all world powers.

Nevertheless, this has been denied by a competent authority. In one of his syndicated Sunday news articles Frank H. Simonds comments on the new Japanese Monroe Doctrine for the Orient as follows: "Today the American people have no desire to engage in war with Japan. On the other hand there is no general perception of the fact that the price of peace is the voluntary renunciation of rights which are alike morally and legally unassailable." And then he counsels the American people to scrap these rights. "To me the very idea of war with Japan is abhorrent and nothing that Japan has done or seems likely to do in the far East, however destructive of American rights and costly to American interests, seems likely to make the game worth the candle. But to escape war it seems to me unmistakable that we must be prepared to scrap rights. And if I am today anxious it is because, unhappily, I do still 'remember the Maine.'"

Unhappily, too, Mr. Simonds forgets or ignores our duties in the Far East. But is he right in his disjunctive premise that either we must scrap rights and sacrifice our interests or wage a war with Japan? There is another alternative and that is the united action of all other signatories to the Nine Power Pact in forcing Japan to acknowledge the legitimate rights, interests, and obligations of other powers in China. Even the Japanese statesmen will yield to such superior power. What we need is an organized body of world opinion functioning to force states desirous of acting on the principle that might makes right to yield to the superior force of those who believe that rights and duties between peoples are ethically and legally determined. Might will cease to make right when the organized moral power of humanity is brought to bear upon those who advocate the doctrine that might makes right. For moral power is more potent in the end than military power. When mobilized it broke the military power of Napoleon in 1815 and of the Central Powers in the World War. And it can break the military power of Japan. Properly mobilized it can do this without war. Mr. Simonds admits that "on the moral side the Japanese course is a challenge to all postwar ideals of international peace," and that "on the material side it is an invasion of the sovereign rights of all other nations." This is equivalent to saying that the Japanese course runs counter to the best moral and legal opinion of the world, and that it stands condemned by the moral judgment of all of the free peoples of the world. The problem, then, is how to make this judgment effective. How can world opinion be mobilized so that it can restrain any one state from making such a challenge and invasion? We will deal with this question in the next chapter.

Assuming that such a mobilization of world opinion is possible, and that the progressive peoples of the earth are willing to acknowledge their obliga-

RIGHTS OF BACKWARD PEOPLES

tions to the backward peoples, what are some of the most elemental responsibilities they would have to accept?

(1) The progressive peoples are under obligation to use the economic resources of the territory of backward peoples for the benefit and uplift of that people. They are entitled to adequate compensation for the services they render, but they have no right to exploit the territory for the benefit of the citizens of progressive states and to the injury of the backward peoples. This is an elemental obligation of progressive peoples correlated with the right of backward peoples to the means for the preservation of their own culture.

(2) The progressive peoples must do everything possible to safeguard and protect the cultures of the backward peoples of the earth. They have no right to impose their own culture, to destroy the language, the folkways, the religious customs, the art of a backward people in the interest of a complete assimilation of that people. The enrichment of humanity can only come about through the preservation and enhancement of all the cultural values men have anywhere achieved on the earth. The wanton destruction of such values in the clashes of peoples during recorded history is a permanent defect in human achievement that can never be blotted out. For example, the lost cultural treasures of the Greeks cannot be recreated. Most of them are gone forever. The same is true of the cultural values of the Iranian civilization. This must never

happen again to those cultural treasures that are now extant anywhere on the earth.

(3) It is the duty of the progressive peoples to train the backward peoples for self-government. To this end they should bend their energies. For this purpose they should use the economic resources they get in administering the affairs of a backward people. And they should gradually withdraw and turn over the administration of affairs to native leaders. This will produce good will and improve all relations between progressive and backward peoples. A deliberate acknowledgment of these obligations, and an honest effort to live up to them would go a long way towards producing an ethical world order.

What to Read

In this chapter I have followed closely W. E. Hocking's *The Spirit of World Politics,* Chs. I, XIV and XV. His book bears the subtitle: *With Special Studies of the Near East.* Part II is entitled: *The Burdens of Egypt;* Part IV, *Mandates: The Burden of Syria;* Part V, *Mandates: The Burden of Palestine;* and Part VI, *B and C Mandates and Colonies.* Each of these discussions is authoritative and informative and of special importance to every student of the rights of backward peoples. See the reports of the Permanent Mandates Commission of the League of Nations for detailed information about the functioning of the various mandates.

See also the *List of Books and Pamphlets relating to the Mandates System and to Territories under Mandate* issued by the mandates section of the League of Nations secretariat.

RIGHTS OF BACKWARD PEOPLES

There is a concise article entitled "Mandate" in the 14th edition of the *Encyclopedia Britannica*. Some books on the mandates are: Norman Bentwick: *The Mandate System;* Julius Stone: *International Guarantees of Minority Rights —Procedure of the Council of the League of Nations in Theory and Practice;* J. Stoyanovsky: *The Mandate for Palestine;* and Freda White: *Mandates.* See the article entitled "Sovereignty of the Mandates," by Quincy Wright in the *American Journal of International Law*, 1923, pp. 691 ff. See also Fannie Fern Andrews: *The Holy Land Under Mandates*, 2 vols.

There is an article on "Treaties" in the 14th edition of the *Encyclopedia Britannica* and the Library of Congress has issued a valuable *List of References on the Treaty-Making Power.* See also D. P. Myers: *Manual of Collections of Treaties and of Collections Relating to Treaties.*

In connection with this chapter a study of the ethical aspects of the Philippine problem may be made. See especially W. C. Forbes: *The Philippine Islands,* 2 vols; E. Hall: *Independence of the Philippines;* R. Palma: *Our Campaign for Independence;* Nicholas Roosevelt: *The Philippines, a Treasure and a Problem;* and Dean C. Worcester: *The Philippines Past and Present.* On our treatment of Indian cultures see William Christie MacLeod's recently published *The American Indian Frontier,* with a valuable bibliography, pp. 565-595, and the classic work by Helen Jackson: *A Century of Dishonor.* See also James H. Tufts: *America's Social Morality*, chap. XIX.

CHAPTER XII

THE NEW LEAGUE OF NATIONS

1. Some Inherent Weaknesses in the League of Nations

The crowning achievement of the makers of the Versailles Treaty was the drafting and adopting of the Covenant of the League of Nations. President Woodrow Wilson was the Chairman of the Commission appointed by the Peace Conference to draft the Covenant, and he was ably assisted by such statesmen as Lord Cecil, General Smuts, M. Leon Bourgeois, M. Venizelos, Colonel House, and others. It was their earnest desire to create an instrument "to promote international coöperation and to achieve international peace and security by the acceptance of obligations not to resort to war, by the prescription of open, just, and honorable relations between nations, by the firm establishment of the understandings of international law as the actual rule of conduct among Governments, and by the maintenance of justice and a scrupulous respect for all treaty obligations in the dealings of organized peoples with one another." This sentence from the prologue to the Covenant indicates the high moral purpose which it was ardently hoped

THE NEW LEAGUE OF NATIONS

the creation of this new international institution would actualize. A little less than a year after the appointment of the Commission, the League of Nations came legally into existence on January 10th, 1920, with twenty-nine of the governments of the earth as members. By 1928 the number of members had risen to fifty-four, some of which have since withdrawn, notably Japan and Germany. Thus for the first time in human history a permanent organization for the application of ethical principles to international relations was effected. Unfortunately, the new institution contained a number of weaknesses which nearly fifteen years of history have clearly revealed.

At the insistence of President Wilson the Covenant of the League of Nations was made an integral part of the Treaty of Versailles, so that the governments in ratifying that document would also accept the Covenant. The creation of the Allied and Associated Powers who had waged the victorious war, it was christened with the blood of their heroes, and forced upon the world by their resolute will, while they were still flushed with the pride of victory. This restricted the League of Nations from the outset and caused all of the enemies of these Allied and Associated Powers to distrust it and to look upon it with suspicion. Moreover, this attitude was shared by some neutral states, so that the League was considerably handicapped from the start. But this handicap was enormously increased by the fact that the Senate of the United States refused to ratify the Treaty of Versailles precisely because it embodied as an integral part the Covenant of the League of Nations. This combined set of circumstances seriously impaired at the outset the effectiveness of an instrument which might otherwise have accomplished its high purpose.

However, there were also other weaknesses inherent in the Covenant itself. It was so drawn as to make the League of Nations weaker than a number of the strongest separate states among its members. Any member can withdraw at any time. The closing section of the last article (26) reads: "No amendments shall bind any Member of the League which signifies its dissent therefrom, but in that case it shall cease to be a Member of the League." Although this section has since been slightly modified it still provides that any member of the League that refuses to accept an amendment automatically ceases to be a member. Such an article is really the death warrant of the League from the standpoint of its effectiveness in dealing with the Great Powers, and as a matter of fact, it never has been strong enough to cope successfully with any of them. In carrying on most of its work the League requires unanimity. Serious differences of opinion among its members have greatly limited the League's power. Then, too, in dealing with the recalcitrant or erring states the League is only able to use persuasion and whatever power publicity may have. Only the member states possess military power. Hence the League has never had anything like adequate power to enforce its actions, and as a matter of fact it never has enforced any important action that it has taken. This has been done by the Great Powers.

2. THE PRESENT STATUS OF THE LEAGUE

It is not surprising that political realists and extreme nationalists have always sought to undermine the influence of the League. In Europe it is commonly held by influential politicians that the world is back where it was in 1914, and that the League is as dead as a doornail. And there are also many Americans who share this view.

One of these critics, Mr. Troyanovsky, Russian ambassador to the United States, in a speech before the American Society of International Law, in April, 1934, is reported by the Associated Press as having said: "Some students are turning to the idea of a supernational support. But they have not been very successful. International law is a collection of the rules directing the relations among the nations. These rules are effective only in so far as the nations themselves accept them, of their own will. The source of the regulating is the nations and not a superforce acting from above the nations. . . . The League of Nations is constituted as a body with equal rights of its members and in substance only unanimous votes are valid, especially since a dissatisfied nation can at any time withdraw from this apparently supernational institution.

"The practical experience with the League of

Nations goes far to prove that my contention is correct, at least for the present time, particularly when some nations regard themselves as supernations destined not to coöperate with others but to dominate and conquer other nations, possibly members of the League of Nations.

"I do not think that one must take too seriously the view which includes under international law moral sense and the laws of human conscience. These influence, of course, international law indirectly, but how could they be directly converted into rules of international law when different nations—and different parts of the populations—have very different views on what constitutes the laws of morals and the dictates of conscience?

"We have to find something more positive, more concrete and definite. I think that only very precise international treaties, duly signed, can give us an acceptable basis for international relations and consequently for international law."

Thus, Mr. Troyanovsky not only attacks the League, but also rejects the basic assumption on which the Covenant of the League is based, and which is implied in the prologue quoted above, namely, that it is possible to apply certain general ethical principles and norms to international relations. He appeals to the fact of the relativity of the moral sense and of moral laws to support his contention that no supernational institution, such as the League of Nations, can ever be effective. What Mr. Troyanovsky overlooks is that treaties and alliances will be considered as scraps of paper unless they are supported by a common sense of justice, which will vindicate their inviolability against any nation that wantonly breaks or disregards them.

Mr. Frank H. Simonds, who in his syndicated Sunday newspaper articles frequently attacks the League of Nations, writes of our being back where we were in 1914, and argues that the League can now be and is being entirely ignored as a factor in international relations. In his article of May 13th, 1934, he refers to the "Wilson affair" as being a "double calamity" since "it created in Europe for the moment a conception of the United States which was totally inexact, and an impression of Europe in America which was without foundations." Europe was disillusioned, embittered, scornful of our rejection of the Treaty of Versailles. The American people think that Wilson was deceived and deluded by Europeans who wanted to exploit American resources. Consequently "on both sides of the Atlantic there is the same sense of having been cheated, deceived, tricked." And again, in his article of June 24th, 1934, Mr. Simonds speaks of the League of Nations as "reeling under the many strokes of recent years," and of Europe as having turned back to the next page of history but one, "thus disposing of the leaf on which Woodrow Wilson wrote his great program for self-determination and a League of Nations to replace the old balance of power and concert of Europe." Elsewhere in the same article Mr. Simonds says: "After the war Woodrow Wilson undertook through his League of Nations to substitute a world council for a European and to admit the small as well as the great powers to the council table. Today, however, the Geneva body is powerless because not less than four of the seven great powers are not members and a fifth—Italy—is hostile. With the United States, Soviet Russia, Japan and Germany out and Italy not a participating member, the league has thus broken down."

However, in spite of what such critics as Mr. Troyanovsky and Mr. Simonds say, and there is certainly some truth in their criticisms, two things are certain. First, the League is not dead, and secondly, it will not die. For it has coördinated many agencies of international coöperation, and created such excellent institutions as the Permanent Court of International Justice and the International Labor Organizations, to the latter of which the United States now adheres. It has actually settled a number of serious political disputes which would have resulted in war had it not been for the prompt and effective action of the League authorities. Among these were the dispute between Sweden and Finland over the Aland Islands, the dispute over the boundary of Silesia, the invasion of Albania, the Corfu incident, the Memel and Mosul disputes, and the Graeco-Bulgar incident. The League has also rendered an immensely valuable service to humanity through its health work, and its restrictions on international opium and white slave traffic. Anyone who is at all familiar with the broad scope of the League's activities, and with the many services which it is rendering to human welfare all over the earth, must admit that a new type of institution has come into being which the greed and avarice and selfishness of the nations will never be able to destroy.

Since the statements of Mr. Troyanovsky and Mr. Simonds, which were quoted above, were made, events have taken a turn more favorable to the League of Nations. Russia has asked admission, has been received into membership, and has been given a place on the Council of the League. Doubtless Mr. Troyanovsky's opinion of this supernational institution is now somewhat less hostile than when he made his address last April. Moreover the League has achieved a notable success in adjusting the serious differences between Hungary and Jugoslavia, which would almost certainly have led to another war in the Balkans. And to this success must now be added the consummation of the Saar plebiscite in accordance with the provisions of the Treaty of Versailles. These important victories have so enhanced the prestige of the League that even Mr. Simonds now says that it would be silly to say that it is dead. In an article in the January, 1935, number of the *Atlantic Monthly* he also admits that the League can function successfully when the great powers are in complete accord, but he predicts that it will again fail whenever a serious difference of opinion arises among the powers represented on the League Council.

Mr. Simonds is undoubtedly right in holding that the League is incapable of settling major disputes among the Great Powers. And this unquestionably means that it is not the League it must ultimately become. A new League of Nations must be constituted out of the beginnings that have been made. Whether this new League comes into existence in time to prevent another World War, or, as Walt Whitman would say, a thousand years from now, come it will, we may rest assured of that. The exigencies of humanity will create the kind of League that organized peoples require for their security.

3. Mr. Baker's Solution of the Present Problem

In an instructive article published in the Summer Number of the *Yale Review* for 1934, Mr. Phillip Noel Baker, a leading British statesman and authority on international law, reviews the notable successes of the League of Nations up to the end of 1931. Then he vividly describes the drift of the nations towards the philosophy of Potsdam and war since September 19, 1931, that being the fateful day when the Japanese war-lords disobeyed their civil governors and began conquering Manchuria. He shows how the advocates of this philosophy have had to shift their ground from emphasizing the doctrine that might makes right to stressing the fear of war. And he argues persuasively that it is the very fear of war on the part of the overwhelming majority of human beings that is responsible for the present drift towards war. This fear is

THE NEW LEAGUE OF NATIONS 255

the only argument armament manufacturers have left in favor of the system of the private production of the implements of warfare, a system which President Roosevelt has rightly said is a grave "source of international discord and strife." The adoption of policies of economic nationalism by every government of the world is due to this fear of war. So also has the serious setback to representative democracy in certain parts of the world been mainly due to this fear. This is especially true of Germany, where the people reached the conclusion "that the new peace system was of no avail, and that they must yield to leaders who would give them armaments in an armed and arming world." Thus the pell-mell rush of the nations to increase their armaments is wholly the result of the fear of war. Even the suppression of minorities is for the purpose of increasing the national unity to prepare for war. "As so often happens in human experience, fear is producing the very thing it fears," says Mr. Baker.

Yet he has not entirely given up hope. He thinks that there are still in Europe powerful spiritual forces which could quickly be turned in the direction of peace by some capable leader. And he thinks that such a leader exists. He argues that Great Britain is the natural leader of the continent of Europe by virtue of being an inevitable part of that continent, and that a number of circumstances "have made Great Britain the present arbiter of fate." But the primal and most vital interest of the British people is peace. Continuing, he says: "They can get it only through the collective system of the League. To get it they must revitalize that system, must make the League strong enough to check aggression, wherever, and whenever it may occur. Accepting Sir Austen Chamberlain's principle that the members of the League 'must be ready to coöperate in the defense of a member which has been wrongfully attacked,' they must seek to establish 'a system which makes it certain that against an aggressor there will be mobilized an irresistible force.' How can that be done? Only by recognizing that since September 19, 1931, Europe and the world have followed the wrong road. Only by recognizing that it was on that day that the new fear of war began. Only by determining that the error then committed shall be made good, that the system which for ten years had succeeded shall henceforward be applied, and that this system shall be strengthened in those points where experience has shown it to be weak. Only by laying before the world a definite program of concrete measures by which this purpose can be fulfilled."[1]

Then Mr. Baker submits his program, every item of which has been thoroughly discussed by the Disarmament Conference, and most of which have been agreed upon by many European governments. This program provides: (1) for the making of war an international crime to which no exception whatsoever shall be allowed, (2) for drastic and

[1] *Yale Review*, Vol. XXIII, p. 679.

effective disarmament, (3) for a pooled security, and for a number of other important restrictions upon all nations, including the strict control of the private manufacture of war material and implements, and the total abolition of all military and naval air forces. This program he calls one "of unlimited international commitments." By adopting such a program Great Britain "can lead the world to peace." And he adds: "The only other alternative is to drift . . . towards the certain prospect of another war."

This great friend of the League of Nations and confident British statesman has not abandoned hope that the present League can be made a real League right now. He says: "It may seem like the wildest paradox to say so at the present moment of confusion, but in many ways it would be far easier to make a real League, to get real disarmament and security, than ever before." And there is no lover of mankind who would not like to think that he is right.

Yet who can believe that Great Britain alone can today assume leadership and exert sufficient power to make the League of Nations a real League, when with their united strength at the moment of victory the Allied and Associated Powers were unable to do so? Great Britain cannot undo the mistakes that were made at Versailles without the full coöperation of the other powers which helped to make those mistakes. It is not the fear of war which is alone responsible for the drift towards war. This drift is partly moral. The injustices that were committed at Versailles, as well as those that have been committed since, must be righted if war is to be prevented. Good will among the nations must supersede envy and hate.

4. THE RECONSTRUCTION OF THE LEAGUE OF NATIONS

Mr. Baker is right in thinking that the road the leading nations have taken recently has been the wrong road. But he does not go far enough. He evidently assumes that the *status quo* established by the Treaty of Versailles was substantially just and can be maintained. But we know that the Allied and Associated Powers blundered when they drafted that treaty. History has abundantly proven some of the arrangements they made to be unworkable in actual practice. Think, for example, of the present pitiful plight of Austria. But the makers of that treaty were not only guilty of the sin of ignorant blundering. Some of the terms of the treaty, as well as certain methods used to force these terms upon the Central Powers, were positively wrong. A few of the delegates knew this at the time, but they acquiesced in the hope that the League of Nations would later correct these errors. Much information has come to light since the Treaty of Versailles was first enforced, proving conclusively that the Allies had made secret agreements to divide certain spoils among themselves. Their adherence to these mutual agreements prevented the making of a just treaty. They were able to coöperate to win the war, but they have not been able to work together in the maintenance of peace. Herein consist the real nest of the wriggling perplexities of the postwar era.

One reason why the American people finally refused to yield to President Wilson's direct and urgent appeal that the United States become a member of the League of Nations was their knowledge of the inequities in the Treaty of Versailles and their reluctance to become entangled in European secret politics. And today there is little hope that public opinion in the United States will support any efforts to make the nation a member of the League. President-emeritus A. Lawrence Lowell, of Harvard University, has well expressed the attitude of informed citizens of the United States towards adherence to the League of Nations in an article entitled "War and the League of Nations," in which he shows clearly why the League is powerless to prevent war. He writes: "We should consult with the League, of course—consult with any association of nations that discusses matters of interest to ourselves as well as to the rest of the world; and do so fully and openly, not clandestinely or with excuses, as if we were a little ashamed to be seen in such company, not as Americans did with their bootleggers in the days of prohibition. But the question of joining the League as a full Member may depend upon what its future is to be. If it shall recover its lost partners, and again become a convention of almost all the nations upon earth—Yes, by all means. But if it is to be a partial body, dominated by England, France, and

Italy, in contrast with other countries whose interests may be divergent, then it will resemble former alliances of some States against, rather than with, others, and the question assumes a different aspect." [2]

Let us return, then, to the suggestion, which was made at the end of Chapter VII, that there be assembled in Geneva or The Hague a World Parliament or congress of distinguished lay (non-political) leaders of all of the peoples living under representative democracies. Let the members of such a parliament or congress be drawn from every division of culture. Assume that only men and women of international reputation in such cultural fields as religion, art, science, education and industry will be selected to sit in such a parliament or congress, and assume that all of its members will have a cosmopolitan outlook and a spirit of tolerance and good will. Once such a body is constituted and actually convenes, let it set to work to reconstruct the League of Nations along the line of a bicameral type of organization in which one house shall consist of representatives of the progressive peoples and the other of representatives of the backward peoples. Having thus reconstructed the League of Nations, let the members of this Congress of the United Free States of the World return to their respective people and appeal to them to ratify their work by governmental action. It is reasonable to anticipate that all agencies within every country that are at all interested in

[2] *The Atlantic Monthly*, July, 1934, Vol. 154, p. 120.

THE NEW LEAGUE OF NATIONS

positive action to outlaw war and to create a new international world order will rally to their support. And with that kind of support there is real hope that the free peoples of the world will be able to force their respective governments to accept the work of such a parliament or congress. Let us have faith enough in the free peoples to believe that they can create a new League of Nations which will be a genuine alliance of all of these peoples with, rather than against, one another.

Following this preliminary congress of all of the free peoples, there should be a new assembly of representatives of all nations to draw up an equitable treaty to settle the issues that today divide the world into a number of armed camps. This new peace and disarmament conference should convene as soon as it can be constituted. Whatever arrangements this world conference is able to work out should then be made a temporary *status quo* to effect a stabilization *pro tem* of all international relations. And the free peoples must agree in advance to enforce an armistice upon any power or powers refusing to accept such a *pro tem* arrangement. During this temporary stabilization the machinery for the new League of Nations must be put into operation, so that there may come into existence a real society of states capable of functioning to guarantee the rights of backward peoples and of minorities, as well as those of progressive peoples.

However, it must be definitely understood that a position of dominance is to be exercised by those peoples who have perfected the institutions of representative democracy and who are now living under that form of government. For only so can the world be made safe for democracy. It is inconceivable that the more than four hundred millions of peoples, living under and enjoying the benefits of representative democratic governments, will ever submit to the domination of any type of dictatorship, be it that of the proletariat or that of some military oligarchy. It is imperative that the new League of Nations have the support of the unified will of the free peoples of the earth. Once it is given this support there will be no power or combination of powers that can resist that general will. Hence the indispensable prerequisite to the making of the new League of Nations is the unification of the will of the free peoples of the earth, under the leadership of the three major powers: France, Great Britain, and the United States.

The free peoples have been too much imposed upon by quack political doctors with their nationalistic nostrums. They have had too many blind and owlishly purblind leaders. They have ceased to understand each other and have even begun to quarrel among themselves. They have lost much of their former enthusiasm for their own political and cultural institutions, just because these very institutions have so frequently been misused by self-seeking grafters to despoil the masses and to empower the unworthy.

What these free peoples need today is some

prophet, like Amos of Tekoa, to thunder forth the eternal message: "Let justice roll down as waters, and righteousness as a mighty stream." They need to give closer heed to the words of the prophet, which have been canonized in Scripture sacred to three great living religions, and which have also been immortalized by George Frederick Handel in his oratorio, *The Messiah:* "Thus saith the Lord of hosts: I will shake all nations; and the desire of all nations shall come." Surely the free peoples must act, and act quickly, to correct the injustices they have done to one another, and to their enemies, and to the helpless backward peoples who are their dependents, so that the desire of all nations for peace and good will may prevail over discord and ill will.

How can they correct these injustices without a new birth of freedom? And how can they obtain this new birth of freedom without a leader? What the free peoples need today is some philosopher, like Plato of Athens, to remind them that "until political greatness and wisdom meet in one, and those commoner natures who pursue either to the exclusion of the other are compelled to stand aside, cities will never have rest from their evils,—no, nor the human race." Someone who unites greatness and wisdom, some dynamic and magnetic western Mahatma who can rally people around the sacred banner of freedom and toleration, as did Voltaire and Burke and Franklin in an earlier age when these priceless ideals were threatened—this is our supreme need. Were such a sagacious democratic leader to come tomorrow he might yet arouse free men and women from their laziness and lethargy; he might revivify and electrify the comfort-loving descendants of the former generations of brave warriors who defied cruel kings and chopped off the heads of merciless despots; he might even fire the virile youth of France and Great Britain and the United States with such fervent zeal for democracy that they would sweep into oblivion the bureaucrats and tyrants, who are darkening counsel in this post-war era through which we are living. But the day after tomorrow it may be too late.

What to Read

There is a permanently valuable article entitled "League of Nations" in the 14th edition of the *Encyclopedia Britannica,* which contains the full text of the Covenant with amendments down to 1929. The first part of this article entitled "Origins and Foundation" was written by Lord Cecil, who represented Great Britain on the League of Nations Commission at the Peace Conference, and the third part entitled "The Work of the First Eight Years" was written by Sir James Arthur Salter, Director of the Economic and Finance section of the League of Nations. Other valuable articles in the same edition are "Europe"; "Security"; "Disarmament"; "Sanctions and Guarantees"; and "League of Nations and Education." The League of Nations issues the following: *Official Journal* and *Supplements; Treaty Series; Monthly Summary,* reports of special commissions, a series of special pamphlets as to special tasks, and a general summary entitled *A Survey.*

On the origin of the League of Nations the following

books are noteworthy: R. S. Baker: *Woodrow Wilson and World Settlement*, 3 vols.; H. Foley: *Woodrow Wilson's Case for the League of Nations;* John H. Latane, editor: *Development of the League of Nations Idea: Documents and Correspondence of Theodore Marburg*, 2 vols.; D. H. Miller: *The Drafting of the Covenant;* and Charles Seymour, editor: *The Intimate Papers of Colonel House*, 4 vols. See also D. J. Fleming: *The United States and the League of Nations;* Sir G. G. Butler: *A Handbook to the League of Nations;* and R. Williams: *The League of Nations Today.* The World Peace Foundation has published a number of works on the League, notably *Handbook on the League of Nations* and *Yearbook of the League of Nations.* See also the special League of Nations number of the *International Journal of Ethics,* Vol. XXXIV, No. 2, January, 1924, and Felix Morley: *The Society of Nations—Ten Years of World Coöperation.* On the World Court see Manly O. Hudson: *The World Court.*

On international coöperation see John E. Harley: *International Understanding—Agencies Educating for a New World* (contains an excellent directory of all agencies working for international understanding); and Spencer Stoker: *The Schools and International Understanding* (contains a full bibliography). A sub-committee of the League has issued *How to Make the League of Nations Known and to Develop the Spirit of International Coöperation.* See also Harry Littell and H. L. Smith *Philosophy of Human Relations, Individual and Collective* (a useful sourcebook containing excerpts from numerous books and monographs), Bulletin of the School of Education of Indiana University, Vol. VII, No. 3, January, 1931; and Alfred Zimmern: *Learning and Leadership.*

The article on *Outlawry of War* in the 14th edition of

the *Encyclopedia Britannica* is especially valuable because it contains the text of the Kellogg Pact. See also Viscount Cecil: *The Way of Peace;* Salvador de Madariaga: *Disarmament;* Charles Clayton Morrison: *The Outlawry of War;* J. T. Shotwell: *War as an Instrument of National Policy;* Frank H. Simonds: *Can Europe Keep the Peace?,* and F. J. Stimson: *The Western Way.*

CASES FOR DISCUSSION

Teachers will find it stimulating to students to devote some time to a discussion of the ethical aspects of specific cases and problems. Such cases are available in current periodicals and each teacher will prefer to select his own material. But from among the numerous cases a few are given below as typical. Many of these can be stated in the form of debate questions, and it would arouse a lot of interest to have some of them debated before student organizations, such as International Relations Clubs or Student Forums, or even in the classroom. Then, too, some of these topics might be assigned for term reports.

1. A lower court refused to grant Professor D. C. Macintosh of Yale University, a citizen of Canada, his request to become a naturalized citizen of the United States, because he wished to qualify the oath of allegiance by refusing to participate in any war as a combatant which he might consider morally wrong. The Supreme Court of the United States upheld the decision of the lower court, but with a division in which Chief Justice Hughes wrote the dissenting opinion. Discuss whether the decision was ethically right, giving specific reasons why you answer as you do. In answering this question, consider the fact that some American citizens, who are conscientious objectors to war, for example, members of the Friends Church, are exempted from

military service. Do you think that it was ethically wrong but legally right? Could this ever be true of any judicial decision? See *United States versus Macintosh,* 1931, Vol. 283, U. S., p. 605.

2. Certain businesses or callings are in legal terminology said to be affected with a public interest. The United States Supreme Court has rendered a number of important decisions in which criteria to determine the meaning of being affected with a public interest have been stated. In the earliest case, *Munn versus Illinois* (1876, 94 U. S., p. 113) grain elevators were held to be affected with a public interest because they exercise a virtual monopoly. In *Brass versus North Dakota* (1894, 153 U. S., p. 391) grain elevators were said to be affected with a public interest on the ground of *legislative enactment.* In *German Alliance Insurance Company versus Lewis* (Kansas) (1914, 233 U. S., p. 389) the court used the twofold test of *indispensable service* and *virtual monopoly.* What ethical considerations would cause the broadening of the meaning of callings affected with a public interest? Do you think the justices of the Supreme Court should be guided by such considerations in reaching their decisions? Apply this to New Deal legislation now under consideration by the Supreme Court, such as the farm mortgage moratorium law and the railroad pension law. Professor Hugh E. Willis discusses the question *When Is a Business Affected with a Public Interest?* in the Indiana Law Journal, Vol. III, pp. 384-390.

3. The National Industrial Recovery Act (NIRA) provided for a number of codes of fair practice for the various industries of the United States. Copies of any of these codes can be obtained from the Government Printing Office at a nominal price. Select one or more typical codes and analyze them to bring out the basic ethical principles which

they embody. Note especially whether they are fair to consumers, producers, laborers, stockholders and other groups affected by their functioning. Do you think it is right for the Federal Government to enforce these codes and treat them as equivalent to laws enacted by Congress? Give reasons for your answer. See Ford P. Hall: *Government and Business* (McGraw Hill Book Co., 1934).

4. The Federal Government is now subsidizing a large number of local community projects such as roads, power plants, sewage plants, waterworks projects, and the National Education Association will soon ask for federal subsidies for local schools. Discuss the ethical problems involved in federal subsidies. For example, should wealth be taken from the states with a large per capita wealth and be used to educate the children in states with a low per capita wealth? This question suggests one ethical problem involved in federal subsidies of local education. What other questions can you suggest and how would you answer them?

5. Discuss whether it would be right or wrong for the Soviet State to acknowledge the foreign debts of the old czarist regime in Russia. Is the United States right in trying to negotiate a treaty with the U. S. S. R. containing an acknowledgment of these debts and a definite policy for paying them?

6. What are the chief ethical considerations involved in the defaulting of the World War debts to the United States by various foreign governments? Should the United States cancel these debts? What ethical problems would be involved in cancelation? Should the foreign governments follow up their temporary defaults with definite notices of repudiation? What about settling the war debts by small token payments, which would acknowledge the debts in prin-

ciple but would reduce payments to nominal sums in each case? What ethical objections might foreign governments make to paying these debts by ceding certain of their colonies that are near the United States? *See War Debts and World Prosperity* by Harold G. Moulton and Leo Pasvolsky.

7. In a number of instances the United States has occupied the territory of small Central American nations, notably Haiti and Nicaragua, to protect the property of American citizens. Sometimes they have policed these countries for months and even years with detachments of marines. Is this type of action morally right? Give reasons for your answer, and try to give some on both sides of the argument.

8. What is the ethical justification for the Monroe Doctrine of the United States? Have we a right to exclude other governments from protecting their interests in the various political regions of North and South America?

9. Do the Japanese have a right to declare a similar policy for Asia? Is the United States ethically consistent in protesting against the Japanese Monroe Doctrine in Asia while maintaining the Monroe Doctrine for North and South America? Give reasons for your answer.

10. Under the terms of the Versailles Treaty the Pacific Islands, which formerly belonged to Germany, were mandated to Japan with the definite proviso that yearly reports were to be made to the Permanent Mandates Commission of the League of Nations. When Japan withdrew from the League, following the publication of the Lord Lytton Report on the Manchurian occupation, she retained control over these islands. This control has recently been protested by the League of Nations. Is it ethically right for Japan to retain possession of these islands in view of the way she ob-

tained them? If not, what do you think would be a just solution of this problem?

11. Analyze the Lord Lytton Report to the League of Nations on Japan's occupancy of Manchuria with a view to discovering and summarizing the basic ethical principles used therein. Can you suggest any ethical defense of the occupancy? Do you find in the report any items which you regard as unfair to the Japanese?

12. Study the Versailles Treaty and draw up a list of its provisions which you regard as unethical. Then draw up a list of the provisions you think were ethical. To put it differently, criticize the treaty so as to bring out its ethical values and defects. Do the same for the Treaty of St. Germain.

13. What ethical problems seem to you to be involved in determining the political allegiance of a province after a war by a plebiscite of the population, conducted under the strict supervision of the League of Nations? In this connection think of the Saar plebiscite. Would it be right to settle the Polish Corridor problem by this method? Why or why not?

14. The establishment of a Jewish national home, in the form of an actual Jewish State in Palestine, has caused a great deal of friction between the Arabs and the Jews. Whether political Zionism is right or wrong has aroused a lot of discussion. In the *Atlantic Monthly,* Vol. 146, pp. 121-132, Professor W. E. Hocking defends cultural Zionism against political Zionism. (See also his *The Spirit of World Politics,* Part V.) In *Foreign Affairs,* Vol. 9, pp. 409-434, Professor Felix Frankfurter states the case for political Zionism. Study these two articles and give your own opinion on this issue. Is political Zionism ethically justifiable in view of the fact that Jerusalem is the sacred city for all three religions: Judaism, Christianity, and Mohammedan-

ism? Would Hocking's suggestion that the region be ruled directly by the League of Nations, and maintained as a place of pilgrimage for adherents of all these religions, be a fairer disposition of Palestine than the building there of a Jewish State under the protection of Great Britain? Give reasons for your answer.

15. Read the article on the *Outlawry of War* in the 14th edition of the *Encyclopedia Britannica,* and write a report on the question of whether war is ethically wrong and should be outlawed as a method of settling disputes between governments and peoples. Is this a realizable ideal in the present state of world politics or a distant goal to be achieved after centuries of human effort?

16. For a number of years Mahatma Gandhi has practiced, and encouraged his people to practice, a policy of passive resistance to the British Government in the effort to secure Dominion status or complete independence for India. Is this identical with the passive resistance taught in the Sermon on the Mount? Is it ethically right for a dependent people to practice passive resistance against an alien government? Give reasons for your answers.

17. A number of nations have agreed to enforce an arms and munitions embargo against two South American nations, Bolivia and Paraguay, in the effort to end a destructive war these governments are waging. Do you consider it just for the great powers to enforce such an embargo against these small republics, while refusing to reach an agreement on limitation of armaments and disarmament among themselves? Has France a right to maintain a vast army while denying Germany the right to rearm? Should the sale of arms and munitions be strictly regulated and completely under the control of some international commission? Should their manufacture be similarly controlled? In this connec-

tion consider the Senate inquiry into the munitions racket in the summer of 1934 and its revelations. See the article by Vita and Joseph Friend entitled "How the Arms Makers Work" in the *Forum,* Vol. XC, pp. 278-285.

18. Discuss the ethical principles involved in the granting of independence to the Filipino people. After independence is granted, should the United States retain a naval base at Manila and exercise a protectorate over the islands? Why or why not?

19. Do you consider the Platt Amendment, which gives the United States the right to intervene in Cuban affairs, to be beneficial to the people of Cuba? Would the United States consider it right for Japan to intervene in the internal affairs of the Filipino people after independence is granted? Are the two cases to be treated the same ethically? Give reasons for your answer.

20. Suppose, as a purely hypothetical case, that the British and United States governments formally protested to Japan for some aggressive action in China by official visits of their ambassadors to the Japanese Foreign Office in Tokio, and then suppose that later the British ambassador returned secretly and informed the Japanese Foreign Secretary that he need not take the protest of his government seriously, since it was made at the request of the government of the United States, would this be ethical? Why or why not? Would this kind of duplicity ever be right for a state?

21. Are secret treaties between governments ever ethically justifiable, and, if so, under what conditions? Should there be a relatively short time limit for all such treaties fixed by international law? Give reasons for your answer.

22. During the years 1903-'04 the British Government sent a military expedition from India to Lhasa, the capital of Thibet, to force the Thibetan authorities to make a commer-

CASES FOR DISCUSSION

cial treaty. A detailed and interesting account of this expedition has been written by Lieutenant L. A. Waddell under the title *Lhasa and its Mysteries, with a Record of the Expedition of 1903-'04*. Discuss whether is was ethically right for the British to send this expedition to Lhasa. Would it always be right for a progressive people to force a backward people to trade with them? Suppose a Mexican Government should come into power that would refuse to trade with the United States, would our government be acting rightly to send a military expedition to force a trade agreement upon such a Mexican Government? Was the expedition into Mexico in pursuit of Villa, during the Wilson administration, ethically justifiable? Give reasons for your answer.

23. The following incident in the Battle of Monterey in the Mexican War is told by Buck Barry, a Texas ranger who participated in the battle.

"Our colonel, seeing our situation, with some of the boys barely yet awake, tried to gain a little time to better prepare us to receive the charge. He rode out front with his saber in his hand and challenged the colonel of the lancers to meet him halfway between the lines to fight a saber fight. Our colonel talked good Spanish, in which the challenge was made. For a moment the burden of suspense and anxiety was very great, while waiting for the conflict between our noble Jack Hays and the commander of the Mexican lancers.

"Hays knew no more about saber fighting than I did, but his object was for the light companies of his regiment to become prepared for the charge of the lancers. So, as soon as the Mexican colonel could divest himself of all encumbrances, he advanced waving his saber, while his horse seemed to dance rather than prance. Within a few feet of the Mexican, Hays pulled a pistol and shot him dead from his horse. This relieved all suspense and anxiety; they charged us like mad hornets." See *A Texas Ranger and Frontiersman,* edited by James K. Greer (The Southwest Press, Dallas, 1932), p. 34.

Considering the fact that this incident happened in a war, do you think the American colonel acted ethically in practicing such deception with the Mexican colonel? Does war automatically suspend ethical principles and make anything right that helps to win the battle? Does the end of winning the war justify any means whatsoever which help to achieve that end? Consider here the use of poisonous gas by Germany in the World War.

24. Should the United States endeavor to conserve the American Indian cultures which now exist on our Indian reservations, or would it be more ethical to distribute their lands to American settlers, and break up the Indian tribes into small groups to be widely scattered over the territory of the United States, with a view to assimilating them into the population as foreign immigrants are assimilated? Give reasons for your answer.

25. Certain national organizations of churches in the United States have gone on record in favor of treating membership in such churches as equivalent to due notice to the government that such a member is a conscientious objector who is opposed to participation as a combatant in any war. If such action becomes general all members of churches will have the same status in wartime that members of the Friends Church (Quakers) now have. In this case do you think the Federal Government is under ethical obligation to respect the opinions of such conscientious objectors by exempting them from military service, as has always been done in the case of Quakers? Or should such exemp-

tion be treated as a privilege which the Government has the right to withdraw at any time? Give reasons for your answer.

26. *The Commission of Inquiry into National Policy in International Relations,* which was appointed by the Social Science Research Council with the approval of President Franklin D. Roosevelt, and of which President Robert M. Hutchins, of the University of Chicago, is chairman, recently made a report to the nation including the following seven specific recommendations:

"1. Continued participation in the disarmament conference, coöperation with the League of Nations in such of its activities as cannot involve us in European conflicts, and adherence to the world court.

"2. Continuance of the present policy in South America and the Caribbean.

"3. Immediate withdrawal from the Philippines on terms that will protect their economic life from injury by American tariffs.

"4. Placing of oriental immigration on a nondiscriminatory basis.

"5. Repeal of the Johnson act.

"6. Immediate settlement of the war debts. We do not believe that the interests of the United States require any payment. Since, however, some countries desire to pay something, we recommend the appointment of a commission with full power to effect settlements.

"7. We recommend that our government make it clear that future investments abroad are at the investor's risk."

Comment on each of these recommendations, bringing out the ethical considerations and implications which each involves. Do you agree with the Commission that the adoption of these policies by our government would relieve "the distrust and tension now prevailing in the world"? If so, does our government's not adopting these policies make the United States partly responsible ethically for this condition of distrust and tension?

27. The League of Nations Union of Great Britain is making a house to house canvass to secure a nationwide expression of opinion on the following five questions:

"1. Should Great Britain remain a member of the League of Nations?

"2. Are you in favor of an all-round reduction of armaments by international agreement?

"3. Are you in favor of the all-round abolition of national military and naval aircraft by international agreement?

"4. Should the manufacture and sale of armaments for private profit be prohibited by international agreement?

"5. Do you consider that if a nation insists on attacking another, the other nations should combine to compel it to stop by (*a*) economic and non-military measures? (*b*) if necessary, military measures?

What value do you think the securing of answers to such questions will have? Would you favor a similar plebiscite in this country?

28. The *Literary Digest* and the *Association of College Editors* are conducting a college peace poll. Here are the questions which each student receiving a ballot is asked to answer yes or no:

"1. Do you believe that the United States should stay out of another great war?

        (a) If the borders of the United States were invaded, would you bear arms in defense of your country?

CASES FOR DISCUSSION

    (b) Would you bear arms for the United States in the invasion of the borders of another country?

"2. Do you believe that a national policy of *an American Navy and Air Force second to none* is a sound method of insuring us against being drawn into another great war?

"3. Do you advocate government control of armament and munition industries?

"4. In alignment with our historic procedure in drafting man-power in time of war, would you advocate the principle of universal conscription of all resources of capital and labor in order to control all profits in time of war?

"5. Should the United States enter the League of Nations?"

Give your own answer to each question and state briefly an ethical explanation of your vote, that is, justify ethically voting as you do.

29. George Catlin (1796-1872) was so great a friend of the American Indians that his critics nicknamed him *Indian-loving Catlin*. In his *Last Rambles,* published in 1868, he gave the following answer to his critics.

"Have I any apology to make for loving the Indians? The Indians have always loved me, and why should I not love the Indians?

"I love the people who have always made me welcome to the best they had. I love a people who are honest without laws, who have no jails and no poor-houses. I love a people who keep the commandments without ever having read them or heard them preached from the pulpit. I love a people who never swear, who never take the name of God in vain. I love a people who 'love their neighbors as they love themselves'!. . . I love a people who have never raised a hand against me, or stolen my property, where there was no law to punish for either. I love a people who never have fought a battle with white man except on their own ground. I love and don't fear mankind where God has made and left them, for they are children. I love a people who live and keep what is their own without locks and keys. I love all people who do the best they can. And oh! how I love a people who don't live for the love of money." (Quoted from George Sarton's article entitled *George Catlin* in *Isis,* Vol. XXII, p. 83.)

Formulate a brief answer such as you think Catlin's critics might have made to this apology. Would you agree with Catlin or with his critics? Explain why.

30. At a meeting of one of the plenary sessions of the Eighth International Congress of Philosophy, which was held in Prague, September 2-7, 1934, there was an interesting occurrence which was reported to the *Journal of Philosophy* (October 25th, 1934) by Professor Ernest Nagel as follows: "Professor Hellpach of Heidelberg, a former Social Democrat and minister of education, pontifically laid down the thesis that *das Volk* is the central subject-matter of sociology, and that common descent and common purposes are constitutive marks of a *Volk*. From this norm for the social sciences he drew the interesting conclusion that every genuine culture is intolerant toward all others. The murmurs of protest from the audience at these words almost drowned out the speaker's voice."

Do you agree with Professor Hellpach's thesis? Do you agree with the conclusion he deduced from it? What conception of ethics do you think is implied in his position?

INDEX

Adamic, Louis, quoted, 212
Admiration, anatomy of, 49
"Affected with a public interest," 267
Alexander the Great and the unity of mankind, 175
Alien control vs. self-government, 211
Allied and Associated Powers, pride of victory, 146-150; and the League of Nations, 247, 257; blunders in drafting treaty, 258
Ambition and the public order, 67
Amos of Tekoa, quoted, 263
Arabs, mandate status, 203; cultural latency, 209
Aristocracy, defined, 82
Aristotle, conception of the state, 31; and the unity of mankind, 174
Armaments, 255, 257; control over, 271
Armistice, monument commemorating signing of, 146; terms, 149
Artel, the, in Russia, 94
Arts, *see* Cultural order
Aryan race, 188, 189
Atkinson, C. F., 192
Atlantic Monthly, excerpt, 40
Augustus, Emperor, 177

Backward peoples, absence of ethics among, 4; theocratic rule, 76; measures of, 203-223; three primary measures, 204; cultural latency, 208; self-government vs. alien control, 211; ethical treatment of, 221; rights, 224-245; right of conquest, 224; economic imperialism, 227; cultural values the basis of right, 233, 243; right to self-government, 235, 244; how it is to be determined, 237; mobilization of world opinion to safeguard, 242; ethical right to force trade with, 273; other measures: ranking of eleven countries, 214; provisional classification of peoples, 218

Bacon, Francis, 31; quoted, 204
Baker, Phillip Noel, on the League of Nations, 254-257
Barry, Buck, 273
Bentham, Jeremy, 173
Bibliography, 19, 42, 62, 79, 102, 125, 152, 179, 201, 222, 244, 264, 267 ff.
Bolshevik government, *see* Soviet State
Bright, John, quoted, 158
Buddhism, doctrine of the brotherhood of men, 198
Business corporations, power of, 139

Campanella, Tommaso, 31
Capitalism and democracy, 139, 144
Cases for discussion, 266-277
Castlereagh's "Conference of Ambassadors," 178
Cataclysm, rejuvenation of a culture by, 195

INDEX

Cavour, Camillo Benso di, quoted, 156
Central Powers, treatment of, in Treaty of Versailles, 258
Century of Progress Exhibition, 141
Chamberlain, Sir Austen, 256
Chamberlin, William H., on Soviet plans, 86; on Russia, 90
China, Japan's attitude toward, 239-242
Christianity, and human slavery, 172; unity of mankind, 178, 198; monistic philosophy, 187
Church, control of, by dictators, 117, 118; and the unity of mankind, 178, 198; *see also* Religion
Cities, Bolshevik, 98
City of the Sun, 31
Civilization, not identical with culture, 182; countries ranked highest in, 214; method of ranking races, 219; *see also* Backward peoples
Classes, growth of, in democracies, 145
Climate, importance of, 160
Codes, ethical, 10
Codes of fair practice, 267
Collectivism in Russia, 94
Commission of Inquiry into National Policy in International Relations, recommendations, 275
Commune, the, in Russia, 94
Communism, aims and ideals, 86, 89, 91-102
Communistic Education of Young Pioneers, 92
Comparative morphology of world history, 193
Competitive values, defined; transformation into non-competitive values, 51; in Soviet State, 94; under dictatorships, 114; in democracies, 134
Comte, Auguste, 173; cultural monism, 190, 191

Conciliar dynastic type of state, 83, 85
Concordia, 176
Concordia Augusta, temple, 177
"Conference of Ambassadors," 178
Congress of the United Free States of the World, 152, 260
Conquering, right and power, 224-227
Conscientious objectors, 266, 274
Conserving force, *see* Force
Consumable goods, *see* Economic goods
Cooperative, the, in Russia, 94
Corporations, business, power of, 139
Corporative state, 107
Corriera della Sera, 124
Covenant of the League of Nations, 246, 250
Criticism, constructive, 56; in Soviet State, 96; under dictatorships, 114; in democracies, 136
Cuba, U. S. intervention, 272
Cultural federalism, 201
Cultural latency, 208, 215
Cultural levels, measures of, 203-223; classification, 214, 219
Cultural monism vs. cultural pluralism, 182-202; defined, 185, 186; monism, 187; pluralism, 192; applications to current international relations, 197-201
Cultural order, 73; relation to private and public orders, 75; basic principles, 77; in Soviet State, 100; under dictatorships, 117; in democracies, 140
Cultural values, 52; the basis of backward peoples' rights, 233-237, 243
Culture, not identical with civilization, 182; as defined by anthropologists, 183; racial theory, 188-189, 191; intolerance toward other cultures, 277

INDEX

Cultures, native, 228, 230
Customs, ethics viewed in relation to, 1; tribal, 2

Debate questions, 266-277
Debt repudiation, 166
Democracies, representative, 82, 84; replaced by dictatorships, 106; cynicism of youth concerning, 112; extent and importance, 129-133; list of self-governing states, 130; application of the four postulates to, 133-137; application of the three orders, 137-143; two criticisms of, 144-146; conclusions, 146-152; plan for a World Parliament set up by, 152, 260; fight against slavery, 173; setbacks due to fear of war, 255; need for leader, 263
Democracy, defined, 82
Dewey, John, 231; quoted, 47, 143, 214 n.; cited, 108
Dictatorship of the proletariat, 85, 144
Dictatorships, extent and uniqueness of, 105-108; in Europe, 106; application of the four postulates to, 108, 111-116; application of the three orders, 108, 116-119; conclusions, 119-125; compared with Sovietism, 121
Diogenes, a cosmopolite, 175
Discussion, cases for, 266-277
Distributive justice, 166
Divorce in Russia, 97
Dixon, R. B., cited, 215
Duggan, Stephen, quoted, 112, 123
Dumas, Alexander, quoted, 156
Duplicity, whether ethical for state, 272
Dynastic type of state, 83, 85, 105

Economic goods, methods of obtaining, 40; competition for, 51; in Soviet State, 94; under dictatorships, 114; in democracies, 134
Economic imperialism, 227-233
Economic value, competitive nature, 37
Economic warfare worldwide, 157
Education, Bolshevik, 91, 93, 100; under dictatorships, 113, 124
Egyptians, civilization and culture, 184
Embargo upon arms, 271
England, democracy, 130, 131
Englebrecht, H. E., cited, 28
Epistle to the Hebrews, quoted, 187
Ethics, and morals, 1; human capacity for ethical reflection, 9; history the story of ideas, 169; ethical idea of freedom, 170, 172; actualization of idea of unity, 174
Ethics, applied, differentiated from theoretical ethics, 1-5; classification of the problems, 5; divisions, 7; examination of the classification, 8; reconstruction of the classification, 11
Ethics, personal, 12; difference between international political ethics and, 166
Ethics, political, 1-21; defined: delimitation of its subject matter, 14-19; principles applied to international relations, 155-181; ethical queerness of states, 160-163; differences between international and personal ethics, 166; plan for building ethical international relations, 224-227
Ethics, professional and business, 12
Ethics, theoretical differentiated from applied ethics, 1-5
European Concert, 178
Evils in the social order, 34-42

INDEX

Existence, continuous, of state, 162
Exploitation, economic, 227-233

Family, the, 66; in Russia, 97; in Italy and Germany, 116; in democracies, 137
Fascism, a unique type of state, 106, 109; youth movements, 111, 117; economic life, 114; freedom of speech, 115; the family, 116; the cultural order, 117; weaknesses, 119; compared with Sovietism, 121; criticism of democracy, 145
Federal subsidies, 268
Fichte, Johann Gottlieb, social consciousness, 28; quoted, 198
Five Year Plan, 91, 92, 96, 98
Fleming, Arthur Henry, 146
Force, conserving, 57; in Soviet State, 96; under dictatorships, 114; in democracies, 136
France, democracy, 130, 131; monument where Armistice was signed, 146; triumph of ethical idea of freedom, 173; cycles in the evolution of, 196
Frank, Doctor, quoted, 188
Frankfurter Zeitung, 125
Freedom, ethical idea of, 170, 174, 178; victory over slavery, 171
Freedom of speech, 56; in Russia, 96; in Germany and Italy, 115, 124; in democracies, 136
Freedom of the press, 96, 124, 136
Frick, Doctor, quoted, 18

Gandhi, Mahatma, 271
Gautier, E. F., cited, 195
Geographical uniqueness of states, 160
Germany, reference to, in Armistice monument, 147; out of League of Nations, 252; *see also* Nazism

Good will, principle of, 165, 167
Goodenough, Edwin R., cited, 174 n., 176
Great Britain, democracy, 130, 131; as leader and a force for peace, 255, 257; military expedition to Lhasa, 272
Great Powers and the League of Nations, 248, 249, 254, 262
Groups, 7, 10; application of ethics to, 12, 14; relations of state to, 15; morality, 18; conflict of the individual with, 37

Hanchin, V., quoted, 92, 98, 100
Handel, George Frederick, quoted, 263
Hays, Jack, 273
Head measurements, 215
Hegel, Georg Wilhelm Friedrich, 231; cultural monism, 189, 191
Hellenistic ideas about, nature of the state, 31; slavery, 171; unity of mankind, 174
Hellpach, Professor, 276
History, the story of ideas, 169; Hegel's philosophy of, 189; Spengler's theory, 192
Hitler, Adolph, 107, 113, 115, 118; suppresses freedom of speech, 115; quoted, 188
Hobbes, Thomas, social contract theories, 32
Hobhouse, L. T., 2
Hocking, W. E., postulates of an ideal state, 45-60; essential rights, 59; quoted, 70, 159, 165, 231 n.; five basic differences between states, 160; on measures of backwardness, 204, 207, 208, 210
Holy Roman Empire, 178
Homonoia, 176
Horse trading, 40
Human beings, *see* Individuals
Human Nature and its Remaking, 46

INDEX

Humanitarianism, relation to patriotism, 25; and the victory over slavery, 172

Huntington, Ellsworth, method of ranking races, 219; rating tables, 220

Hutchins, Robert M., 275

Huxley, Thomas Henry, quoted, 101

Hyde Park, freedom of speech in, 136

Ideals, clash of, 36; interested and disinterested, 49

Ideals, identical, 47; and the Soviet State, 91; and dictatorships, 111; and representative democracies, 133

Ideals, moral, subservience of political actions to, 169

Ideas, Dewey on lack of, 143

Identity and continuity of states, 161

Imperialism, economic, 227-233

Indians, treatment of, 224, 226, 228, 274

Individuals, as direct moral agents, 7, 10; application of ethics to relations of, 11; moral behavior, 18; relation of state to, 14; relation of state to, 22; conflicts with groups, 36-42; sacrifice of, for state, 109

Institute of International Education, excerpt from *News Bulletin*, 123-125

Institutions, fixity and rigidity, 38, 56; conserving values of, 57

Internal social organization, flexibility, 217

International Humane Society, 221

International Labor Organizations, 252

International law, 159, 246, 249

International relations, ethical judgments on, 11; application of ethical principles to, 155-181; ethical queerness of states, 160-163; relations of states since World War, 164; actualization of idea of unity of mankind, 174-179; League of Nations, 178, 246-266; applications of cultural monism and pluralism to, 197-201; plan for building ethical relations, 239-244; recommendations of Commission of Inquiry into National Policy, 275

Internationalism, goal of, 197-200

Islamic culture, 209

Italy, *see* Fascism

James, William, 231

Japan, attitude toward China, 239-242; out of League of Nations, 252; Pacific Islands mandated to, 269; occupancy of Manchuria, 269, 270

Japanese Monroe Doctrine, 239, 241, 269

Jerusalem and political Zionism, 270

Jewish state in Palestine, 270

Jews, Nazi opposition to, 118

Jural postulates, 59-62, 79

Kant, Immanuel, 231; classification of problem of philosophy, 5; ethical theory, 6; postulates of morality, 45; quoted, 109, 110

Knowlson, T. Sharper, quoted, 185

Kossovo epic, 213

Labor and the League of Nations, 252

Lamaseries of Thibet, 76, 217

Law of the three stages, 190

League of Nations, earlier movements, 178; nations admitted to, 219; the new League, 246-

266; inherent weaknesses, 246; birth and membership, 247; attitude of United States, 248, 251, 259; present status, 249; activities and services: disputes settled, 252; Baker's solution of present problem, 254; three-part program, 256; reconstruction of League, 258; by a congress of free peoples, 260; Pacific Islands mandate, 269

League of Nations Union of Great Britain, questionnaire, 276

Legal persons, 7

Lenin, Nikolay, aims and ideals, 86, 92

Lhasa, expedition to, 272

"Liberal State," 145

Liberty, right to, 59

Liberty and Democracy, excerpt, 150

Lincoln, Abraham, quoted, 146, 174

Locke, John, 173

Lord Lytton Report to League of Nations, 269, 270

Love, principle of, 65

Lowell, A. Lawrence, quoted, 259

Machiavelli, Niccolò di Bernardo, quoted, 155

Macintosh, D. C., 266

MacIver, Robert M., classification of states, 82, 105, 129; on the Soviet State, 85

Manchuria, Japan's occupancy of, 270

Mandated countries, 203, 218, 227

Manifest destiny, 229

Marett, R. R., quoted, 191

Marxian philosophy, 86, 100, 190, 191, 200; as opposed to democracy, 144

Masses, condition of, a measure of backwardness, 207, 215

Mastery of nature a measure of progress, 204, 215

Mayan culture, 208

Mein Kampf, 115; excerpt, 188

Mercy, value of, 149, 150

Mexican War, unethical incident, 273

Mexico, conquering power over, 224, 226

Might makes right, principle of, 156, 225, 228, 238

Military service, exemption from, 266, 274

Monarchial oligarchy, 84

Monarchy, defined, 82

Monism, cultural, *see* Cultural monism

Monroe Doctrine, justification for, 269

Monroe Doctrine, Japanese, 239, 241, 269

Monterey, Battle of, incident, 273

Moral agents, direct, 7, 10

Moral ideals, subservience of political actions to, 169

Moral power, potency of, 242

Morality, in individuals and groups, 18; postulates of, 45; level of, a measure of progress, 205, 215

Morals, distinction between ethics and, 1

More, Sir Thomas, 44

"Mores make anything right," 1, 3, 204

Municipal law, 7 n., 10, 159

Munitions, production of, 255; control, 257; embargo upon, 271

Mussolini, Benito, 106, 113, 115, 117, 118

National Industrial Recovery Act, codes, 267

Nationalistic-socialistic states, 106

Native cultures, 228, 230

INDEX

Native's Return, The, excerpt, 212

Nature, mastery of, a measure of progress, 204, 215

Nazism, a unique type of state, 106; youth movements, 111, 148; economic life, 114; freedom of speech, 115; the family, 116; the cultural order, 117; weaknesses, 119; compared with Sovietism, 121; Nordic Myth exploited by, 188; cultural monism, 189

Negro music and literature, 213 n.

Neue Freie Presse, 124

New Atlantis, The, 31

Nine Power Pact, 240, 241

Non-competitive values, 52; transformation of competitive values into, 51; in Soviet State, 94; under dictatorships, 114; in democracies, 134

Non-resistance, 167

Nordic Myth, 188

Norms in ethics, 3

Oath of allegiance, qualification of, 266

Oligarchic type of state, 83, 85, 105

Olympic Games, 138

Orders of an ideal state, 64-79; application to Soviet State, 97-102; to dictatorships, 108, 116-119; to democracies, 137-143

Pacific Islands mandated to Japan, 269

Parliament, World, 152, 260

Passive resistance, 271

Paternalism in democracies, 133

Patriotism, 23, 24, 25

Peace Conference and the League of Nations, 246

Peace treaty, *see* Versailles, Treaty of

Peasants, Bolshevik, 94

Permanent Court of International Justice, 252

Personal ethics, *see* Ethics

Philippine Islands, right to native culture, 234; relation of U. S. to, 272

Philosophers, classical, conceptions of state, 30

Philosophy, classification of problems of, 5; basic questions, 7; examination of the classification, 8

Plato, ideal state, 31; cited, 56; conception of human soul as rational, 170, 171; attitude toward slavery, 171; unity of mankind, 174; quoted, 263

Platt Amendment, 272

Play institutions in democracies, 138, 139

Plebiscites, 270

Pluralism, cultural, *see* Cultural monism vs. Cultural pluralism

Political ethics, *see* Ethics

Political monism vs. political pluralism, 186 n.

Political realism, 155

Politico-economic institutions, 69

Polytechnic education, 93, 100

Pope, controversy with Mussolini, 117, 118

Postulates, jural, 59-62, 79

Postulates of an ideal state, 44-62; application to the Soviet State, 91-97; to dictatorships, 108, 111-116; to representative democracies, 133-137

Postulates of morality, 45

Pound, Roscoe, jural postulates, 60-62, 79; cited, 120

Power-over and power for, backward peoples, 231

Pride of Allies, harmful effects, 146-150

Private order, 64; relation to public order, 70, 78; to cultural order, 76; application to Soviet State, 97; to dictatorships, 116; to democracies, 137

Private property, in the Soviet State, 94; under dictatorships, 114
Proclamation of democracy, 150, 152
Professional and business ethics, 12, 13, 15
Professional institutions, 15
Proletariat, dictatorship of, 85, 144
Property of states, 162
Provincialism, 23, 24, 25
Ptolemaic theory of history, 192
Public morality, level of, a measure of progress, 205, 215
Public order, 67; relation to private order, 70, 78; relation to cultural order, 75; application to Soviet State, 99; to dictatorships, 117; to democracies, 139

Quigley, Hugh, quoted, 118

Races, backward, *see* Backward peoples
Racial theory of culture, 188-189, 191
Ratzel, stresses importance of climate, 160
Recreational activities, *see* Private order
Reading lists, 19, 42, 62, 79, 102, 125, 152, 179, 201, 222, 244, 264, 267 ff.
Realism, political, 155
Reflective morality, 3
Religion, and the cultural order, 74, 76; in Soviet State, 100; under dictatorships, 117, 118; under democracy, 141; unity of mankind a teaching of, 178, 198
Representative democracies, *see* Democracies, representative
Republic of Plato, 31, 175
Revolution, World, of Communists, 86, 92

Right of conquest, 224-227
Rights, essential, 59; states are subjects of, 165; of backward peoples, 224-245
Rocco, Alfred, quoted, 109, 131
Roman Empire and the unity of mankind, 177
Roosevelt, Franklin, D., quoted, 240, 255, 275
Rousseau, Jean Jacques, social contract theories, 32
Rowell, Chester, quoted, 122
Royce, Josiah, cited, 23
Russell, Bertrand, 231
Russia, technique of "getting on" in, 40; condition of people, 90; Bolshevik aims and ideals, 91-102; education, 93; and the League of Nations, 252, 253; *see also* Soviet State

Samuel, Sir Herbert, quoted, 131
Savages, *see* Backward peoples
Science, *see* Cultural order
Scott, Sir Walter, quoted, 23
Secret treaties, 272
Security, right to, 60
Self-government, vs. alien control, 211; right to, 235-237, 244; how determined, 237-244
Sellars, Roy Wood, 231
Senate, U. S. and League of Nations, 247, 252, 259
Serbs, Turkish domination, 212
Shakespeare, quoted, 67, 149
Simonds, Frank H., quoted, 241, 242; attitude on League of Nations, 251, 253
Sims, William Snowden, quoted, 157
Slavery and the ethical idea of freedom, 170-174
Social consciousness, birth, 22; stages in development of, 25-35; of Whitman, 25; of Fichte, 28
Social Contract, quoted, 33

INDEX

Socialistic state a Soviet ideal, 86, 89, 92
Socrates, 31, 56
Soul, Platonic doctrine, 170, 171; Christian doctrine, 172
Sovereign states, *see* States
Sovereignty of dictatorial state, 109
Soviet State, classification, 85; based upon principle of violence, 85, 92; socialistic ideals and plans, 86, 89, 92; opposing interpretations of the importance of, 87-91; application of the four postulates to, 91-97; application of the three orders, 97-102; compared with Nazism and Fascism, 121; with democracy, 145; reasons for success, 132; question of debts of the czarist regime, 268; *see also* Russia
Spengler, Oswald, theory of cultural pluralism, 183, 184, 186, 192, 196
Spinoza, Benedict, 29; conception of the state, 32; classification of states, 82
Spirit of World Politics, The, 160
State of estates, 107
"State of nature," 32, 33
States, sovereign, ethics and relations between, 11, 12; relation to individual members, 14; to groups, 15; relations between: backwardness and progressiveness, 16; why there are states, 22-43; relation to citizens, 22; nature of, 30; conceptions of classical philosophers, 31; theories of Hobbes and Rousseau, 32; three kinds of evils, 34-42; elementary forms, 35; actual *vs.* ideal, 41-42; utopias, 44; postulates of an ideal state, 44-62, 91-97, 108, 111-116, 133-137; three orders of an ideal state, 64-79, 97-102, 108, 116-119, 137-143; conformity of actual to ideal: the problem state, 81; Spinoza's three types, 82; MacIver's classification, 82-84, 105, 129; the Soviet State, 85-104; dictatorships, 105-128; nationalistic-socialistic, 106; totalitarian, 118, 145; representative democracies, 129-154; ethical queerness: the five basic differences, 160-163; geographical uniqueness, 160; identity, 161; property: continuous existence, 162; vital interests, 163; relations between, since World War, 164
Stoic ideas of the unity of mankind, 176
Supreme Court cases for discussion, 266, 267

Tapeworm theory of history, 192
Tarn, W. W., cited, 174 n., 175; quoted, 176, 177
Taylor, Griffith, cited, 215
Teachers under dictatorships, 124
Temple of the Imperial Concord, 177
Ten Kate, H., criteria for ranking countries, 214
Theocratic orders, 76; in Thibet, 217
Theophrastus, quoted, 176
Thibet, Lamaism, 76; theocratic social order, 217; British expedition to, 272
Tiberius, Emperor, 177
Totalitarian state, 118, 145
Trade unions under dictatorships, 123
Treaties, secret, 272
Treaty of Versailles, *see* Versailles, Treaty of
Tribal customs, 1, 2
Tribal organization, 35
Troyanovsky, Ambassador, quoted, 249

Truth, suppression of, 122
Turkey, status of women, 117

Union of Socialist Soviet Republics, *see* Russia: Soviet State
United States, attitude toward League of Nations, 247, 252, 259; Monroe Doctrine, 269
United States vs. Macintosh, 266
Unity of mankind, idea of, 174-179; actualization of idea, 191; an ideal of the cultural monists, 197-200; cultural federalism, 201
Utopias, 44

Versailles, Treaty of, 148-150; treatment of backward peoples, 203, 218, 227, 229; and the League of Nations, 246, 247; refusal of United States to ratify, 248, 251, 259; injustices committed, 257; Pacific Islands mandated, 269; ethical values and defects, 270
Violence and the Soviet State, 85, 92
Vital interests of state, 163

Wangling, 40
War, fear of, and its consequences, 254, 257; outlawry of, 256, 271; ethical principles, 274

War to end war, probability of, 150, 152
Wealth, pursuit and power of, 53
Wesleyan religious revival, 173
West European culture, 193, 195
Westermarck, Edward, 2
Whitehead, A. N., cited and quoted, 15, 165, 168-174
Whitman, Walt, social consciousness, quotations, 25-28, 137
Wilde, Norman, quoted, 35
Wilson, Woodrow, 224; war slogans, 148; and the League of Nations, 246, 247, 251, 252, 259
Women, status in Russia, 97; in Italy and Germany, 116; in Turkey, 117; under democratic government, 138, 139
World opinion, mobilization of, 242
World Parliament, 152, 260
World revolution of Communists, 86, 92
World War, probability of new, 150, 152

Youth, conception of the state, 22
Youth movements under dictatorships, 111, 148
Yucatan, Mayan people, 208

Zionism, political, 270